Charlotte

A Holocaust Story of Strength, Courage, and Hope

By

Charlotte Adelman
and Mala Blomquist

Charlotte: A Holocaust Story of Strength, Courage, and Hope

Copyright ©2025 by Charlotte Adelman and Mala Blomquist

Cover Design: Jeremy Goldberg (grandson) and Christian Dalonzo
Editors: Mary L. Holden, Jacob Goldberg (grandson) and Mylan
Blomquist
Copyright: Charlotte Adelman and Mala Blomquist
Interior Design: Artline Graphics

ISBN print 979-8-9900761-9-8
ISBN ebook 979-8-9900761-8-1
ISBN audible 979-8-9900761-7-4

DEDICATION

To the memory of my Maman, Rajzla Rosencwajg, who smothered me with love until the age of ten, when she was taken by the Nazis. She would have loved to know that my dream of becoming an American came true.

To my Papa, Herszle Rosencwajg, who was crazy about me and always put me first. He protected me from harm and gave me the freedom to live my life the way I always wanted.

In loving memory of my beloved husband, Alex. For 50 years, he listened to my story with compassion and never tired of hearing it. In his eyes, I could do no wrong. He was the love of my life, and I will cherish the memories we made together forever.

To Roz, Marc, and Seth,

During my darkest days in the cellar, I would dream of being married and having a little girl and a little boy. My dreams came true! I am so proud to be your mom. Roz and Marc, and my son-in-law, Seth, I love our relationship and all the memories we have shared together. I am forever grateful.

To my precious grandchildren, Jeremy and Jacob,

In the cellar I dreamt of having two children, but never that I would have two such wonderful grandchildren. You give me the strength to continue to live my life. I enjoy our time together and love seeing you live your dreams. Thank you for making sure we always have dessert and indulging me in four kisses!

To my family and friends,

Always remember that you are loved and cherished. I wrote this book to show the power of love, family, and resilience. Continue to live your lives with positivity, respect, and hope.

With all my love, now and forever,
Charlotte

Dedication

To my family, thank you for your endless love, support, and belief in me, even when I doubted myself.

To Charlotte, who is also family, thank you for entrusting me with your remarkable story.

Mala

ACKNOWLEDGMENT

I would like to extend my sincere appreciation to the Phoenix Holocaust Association, USC Shoah Foundation, Arizona Jewish Historical Society, and Mémorial de la Shoah for their invaluable support and resources. Their dedication to preserving the history and stories of Holocaust survivors and their families ensures that we are never forgotten.

I would like to extend my heartfelt gratitude to the Quatreville family and the Elazare family who put their lives at risk to keep me safe. Your bravery is the reason I am here today. I also want to express my appreciation to the janitor who helped me send a telegram to Madame Elazare, an act of kindness that has never been forgotten. Thank you to the Fragman family for giving me a home after the war and a chance to rebuild my life. I am forever grateful.

I want to express my deepest gratitude to Mala Blomquist, who spent every Sunday with me to bring my story to life. Your trust and love eased the pain of recounting my story. Thank you, Mala, for your dedication and passion to the memory of my family.

Lastly, thank you to the entire Community Voices team at Meta for arranging and documenting the most beautiful trip to France to reunite with Alain and his family. It was a magical experience and one I will never forget.

CONTENTS

FOREWORD

"And though she be but little, she is fierce."
William Shakespeare's A Midsummer Night's Dream

It didn't take long after I first met Charlotte Adelman for the above quote to enter my mind. She stands quite shy of five feet tall, and her eyes flash with a spark that burns deep within.
We would meet on Sunday mornings at the dining room table in her cozy home, where she raised her children and lived with the love of her life, Alex, until his death.

Before we started, she always pushed the bowl of wrapped chocolates on the table toward me. "Take one," she would say. I would tell her that was my reward when we were done for the day.

For the next hour, I would ask her questions, and she would be forced to return to that horrific time during the Holocaust. Some stories were repeated, others coming through with new details deep in her memory as if stored at the bottom of a chest, only pulled out when she was ready to open them and say the words out loud.

After our time together, Charlotte always planned on being with family, playing mahjong, or gathering for dinner. This was emotionally draining for her, and even though the stories never left her mind, having someone press you for details is overwhelming.

She would always walk me to the door, parting with a hug, and come out and stand on her front porch to make sure I got in my car safely and pulled away. Sometimes, I would have to pull over in her neighborhood, stop the car, and openly sob over something she had shared with me. I tried to be strong in front of her, but there were days when the sheer power of her words and what she endured were too much to take.

I first met Charlotte in 2018 when I interviewed her for an article I was working on. While she shared the same information she has delivered to thousands of schoolchildren over the years, I was taken aback by her resilience and optimism. Her story stuck with me.

Her daughter, Roz, was also at that first meeting. I had written about other events in the community and would run into Charlotte, and we became friends. One day, Roz asked me if I knew anyone who could write her mother's memoir. I told her I would make a few calls and see who I could find for the job.

After I hung up, I thought of local authors I had met, and then I had a constant gnawing in my gut that grew over a few days. I called Roz back and told her I wanted to write the book. I told her I had no prior experience writing a book but would like the chance. She agreed and knew that Charlotte felt comfortable with me, so we began our Sunday morning meetings that lasted for years, only taking time off from meetings for holidays and when the pandemic hit.

On the pages where you see a bold indented section, these are Charlotte's own quotes pertaining to the story being told in that section. Even though the story is a compilation of all her words, I wanted to include her thoughts while she was sharing a particular memory.

All too soon, we are going to lose these survivors who witnessed the horrors of humanity, losing their families and loved ones, only to find the strength to overcome enormous obstacles as they rebuilt their lives from nothing.

This is just one survivor's story; there are countless more.

CHAPTER ONE

An Idyllic Beginning

Charlotte Rozencwajg struggled with the heavy wooden dining chair to perfectly position it for the best view out of the giant picture window that spanned the front of her family's Paris apartment. Satisfied with her vantage point, she plopped down on the floral brocade upholstery, and let out a contented sigh. In front of that window was the seven-year-old's favorite spot. She loved to watch the activities at the Catholic church across the street, Église du Bon-Pasteur de Paris, and the people rushing along on the sidewalk below, imagining where they were going and what treasures were contained in their shopping bags.

"What's going on in the neighborhood today?" Charlotte's mother, Rajzla, asked her daughter as she ran her fingers gently through the girl's hair.

Charlotte looked up at her mother and smiled as they both watched the people together.

The Rozencwajgs lived in a modern building for the 1930s. Their apartment was situated directly above a bakery; living quarters started on the second floor of the building, with the first floor comprised of shopfronts lining the Rue de Charonne. The neighborhoods in Paris are divided into arrondissements (administrative districts) that branch out in a clockwise spiral from the center of the city, starting in front of Notre Dame, and are numbered from one to 20. The Rozencwajg's apartment was in the 11th arrondissement, a highly populated neighborhood that was home to many Jews.

Paris enjoyed a period of *les années folles*, "the crazy years," in the decade of the 1920s following the end of World War I. The city experienced an economic boom as hope for the future was restored in its residents. People once again flocked to the theater, music halls, dance halls, and museums. Its strong economy and culture attracted people from across Europe who were looking for a new beginning in the "City of Light."

Charlotte's parents, Rajzla (née Wajcberg) and Herszla (Herszle) Rozencwajg, were two of those seekers of a new beginning. They each had a cousin who had moved to Paris, and in their correspondence with the men, they described the successes they were enjoying. Lazar Balderman, her mother's cousin, was a tailor. Mayer Shafer, her father's cousin, owned a thriving kosher restaurant. Both men gave descriptions of the large, welcoming, vibrant Jewish communities.

"You must come to visit us in Paris. It is magnificent," wrote Lazar.

"My restaurant is always packed, and we have people that have welcomed us here," Mayer shared.

At the time, Rajzla and Herszle were living in Lodz, Poland. The second-largest Jewish community in the country, after Warsaw, Lodz had become a large industrial center. By the end of the 19th century, Lodz grew into a hub of industry and a leader in manufacturing clothing, metals, chemicals, and paper. More factories were built to keep up with the increase in manufacturing, and these factories needed a large workforce to run them. People began coming to Lodz for the chance of employment, even if the working conditions were not optimal. By 1913, the population of the Polish town surged to nearly 500,000.

Rajzla and Herszle both came from large families. Herszle was one of 10 children, and Rajzla was one of nine. Herszle was of slight build, a hard worker with calloused hands and a quiet soul, but he could become confrontational when pushed. He also had the gift of foresight. He would often take chances because he felt sure of the outcome. Rajzla was the opposite of her husband when it came to taking chances or being argumentative. She preferred to play it safe and steer clear of trouble. Rajzla, petite, with dark hair and alabaster skin, seemed fragile, although she was stronger than she appeared to be.

Many families in Lodz took advantage of the influx of new residents and created small businesses that they ran out of their homes. Herszle's Orthodox Jewish parents were no exception; they ran a successful wholesale produce business. In his youth, Herszle helped with the business, working after school and on the weekends. After his father died suddenly, he was forced to take over selling fruits and vegetables, and dealing with vendors. Although he knew he needed to do whatever was necessary to help his mother and support the family, he never felt in his heart that his future lay solely in running the family business.

Herszle set his sights on attending law school, but a serendipitous meeting one afternoon changed his career path and his entire future. Running late for school one morning, he decided to take a shortcut across a field that involved jumping a low fence. In his haste, he didn't clear the fence completely and caught his trousers on a nail, causing a small tear.

Knowing that he would get reprimanded by his mother for his torn trousers, Herszle decided to visit the tailor, Mr. Friedman, on his way home from school. He entered the tailor's small shop and Mr. Friedman looked up. "Hello, Herszle," he said. "What brings you in today?"

"I was being careless, and I tore my pants. Can you fix them, please?"

The tailor stopped what he was working on and made the repair. Herszle had been in the shop before, but he had never noticed all the different tools of the tailor's trade. The afternoon light played off the metal of the various scissors, needles, and thimbles lined up in perfect order; the folds of fabric next to the sewing machine revealed textures and patterns Herszle had never seen before.

Herszle watched the man repair his pants, taking great care in such a small task. Mr. Friedman worked in silence, his face taking on a light-hearted steadfastness. The edges of his mouth were drawn up in a slight smile while he worked. Herszle had never seen anyone find such joy in their work and he was so impressed by Mr. Friedman's passion for his craft that he decided then and there that he wanted to become a tailor. That change of heart turned out to be quite fateful because if he had pursued law, he would never have been able to teach his new bride how to be a seamstress, thus creating a successful business they could work at together.

It had been more than a decade since the end of World War I, and Rajzla and Herszle noticed changes in the ways Jews were treated in Lodz. It was subtle at first, but then the situation escalated. Discriminatory laws were enacted, and signs of growing antisemitism were everywhere they went. When they were younger, they heard about the violent riots—the pogroms—by people against Jews and Jewish-owned businesses, and the couple feared this would happen again. They wanted to move away from the threats, somewhere with a robust Jewish community, somewhere they could start, and raise, a family.

It was Herszle who started the conversation. "My love, I think it's time that we leave Lodz and go somewhere new."

"Where would we go?" Rajzla asked. She was not as quick to embrace change as her husband, and the thought of moving away from family made her nervous.

"I was thinking of Paris. We have some family there, and from our cousins' letters, it looks like a good place for Jews."

So, when the Rozencwajgs wrote to their cousins about their thoughts of leaving Lodz, they received replies wholeheartedly encouraging them to move. It seemed right, and the couple decided that moving would be an opportunity. Much to the rest of their family's dismay, they left Poland.

When they'd settled in Paris in late 1929, they decided to stick with what they knew best. The young couple set up a tailoring business inside their cramped two-room apartment and felt happy in their new life.

Their happiness grew one spring morning—on March 26, 1932—when they welcomed their first child, a daughter named Charlotte. Rajzla and Herszle were overjoyed as Charlotte's birth further established their new beginning in France. Now with a baby in their home and workplace, they realized their family needed more space. When Charlotte was nine months old, they moved into an apartment at 166 Rue de Charonne. This living space had high ceilings and was filled with light that poured in from an enormous picture window that looked out upon the busy street below.

"We lived in a gorgeous building, a special building; you didn't see those kinds of buildings in Paris in the 1930s. It was very, very modern, with toilets and showers in the apartments, hot water, an incinerator for the trash on every floor, and an elevator."

The apartment complex consisted of four separate towers, A through D, and each tower had 10 floors. On each floor, there were 10 apartments. Three of the buildings were connected by an enormous concrete rooftop terrace. All the children who lived in those buildings used the rooftop terrace as a playground. Parents felt it was safer than having the children play in front of the building near the busy street. The terrace had metal railings and a grating that ran all along the perimeter, preventing little ones from getting too close to the rooftop's edge. The tenants in those buildings were 90 percent Jewish and Charlotte knew about 30 children close in age as playmates. Every day was like a party with her friends.

Charlotte was always so excited for playtime that she had difficulty sitting still to eat. Her mother's voice sounded stern as she pushed the girl back into her chair. "Charlotte, you can't go up to play until you finish your breakfast!"

After shoveling the rest of her breakfast into her mouth, Charlotte grabbed her mother's hand and said, "Let's go!" Freed from the chair, Charlotte rushed past her mother into the hallway. Since she never had the chance to ride the elevator to her first-floor apartment, Charlotte loved when she could take the elevator to the terrace to play.

Charlotte gained another playmate when the family welcomed a son. Max Henri was born in 1938, six years after Charlotte.

"He was named after my mother's father and my father's father. His full name is Max Henri. His nickname was Riri, and even now I call him Riri. He couldn't say Max or Henri, so when they would tell him his name was Max Henri, he would mumble 'Riri.'"

Rajzla, known as Rose to her neighbors because she decided it sounded more French and less Jewish, was very protective of her children, especially Charlotte. She would never let them go up to the terrace alone. Often, Rajzla was the only adult watching over the children playing. The other parents trusted her and knew she would be up on the terrace making sure all the kids were safe, not just her own.

Eventually, when she'd told enough people that Rose was her name, she stopped using Rajzla altogether. She liked the name Rose because Herszle's pet name for her was Róza, the Polish word for rose.

Charlotte also was given a nickname by the children. Many of them couldn't say Charlotte. They heard her mom call her "Lolotte," but finding that also hard to pronounce, they simply called her "Lola."

Under her mother's watchful eye, Charlotte played hopscotch on the terrace. One child had a tricycle, which children stood in line and waited to take turns riding across the smooth cement. Most of the children had dolls, but since her family didn't have extra income to spend on toys, Rose made dolls for Charlotte from empty wooden spools that held thread.

"I had several dolls made of spools. When I would visit my friends, they would have dolls, and I would have the spools. They would fight to get my dolls because they never saw anything like that. My mother was a beautiful sewer and made beautiful clothes for the spools."

On one birthday, Rose said, "Lolotte, I have a special surprise for you." Because Rose felt terrible that her daughter didn't have any "real" dolls to play with like the other girls, she purchased a Dionne paper doll set for Charlotte.

"Oh mama, I love them!" said Charlotte as she gently took the paper dolls out of their wrappings. She cherished that gift and thought they were the best dolls she ever had.

The Rozencwajgs spoke Yiddish at home, and occasionally Polish, when there was something they did not want Charlotte to overhear. She was learning French in nursery school and would come home and try to teach her parents a few French words or phrases.

"I taught my parents a little French, but my father picked it up better than my mom. When we would go to the subway, my mom would speak in Yiddish, so I would pull her skirt and say, 'Not here, momma!' because I was ashamed that she didn't know French. I would talk and she would listen."

Charlotte's best friend was Betty Elazare. Betty lived in the building, but her mother was very strict and would not let her go up to the terrace to play. The two friends attended nursery school together. Betty was often jealous of Charlotte because of the way she made friends so easily. Everyone loved her. She was also the favorite student of her teacher, Mademoiselle Peron. Not to mention that there was a boy in nursery school that Betty liked, but he liked Charlotte more.

When not playing with friends on the terrace, Charlotte played underneath the wooden dining room table that doubled as a worktable while her mother and father sewed. Herszle did most of the garment construction and Rose would do the finer finish work.

Often, while working, the Rozencwajgs sang songs they knew from attending synagogue on Saturdays. One song was a Jewish prayer that Herszle changed the words of to sing in Yiddish just for Charlotte: "Where is the home, where is the village, where is that little girl that I love so much? Here is the home, here is the village and here is the little girl that I love so much."

The bulk of the couple's work came from special orders, sometimes from their neighbors.

One of them, Madame Roland, lived on the third floor. She was a good customer and often placed orders for the same item in multiple colors. Madame Roland was one of the few non-Jews in the building, and she became very fond of the Rozencwajgs. In fact, everyone was fond of the Rozencwajgs. If any of their neighbors ever needed anything, they knew they could go to them. When someone needed a sitter for their children, they came to Rose.

One day a distraught neighbor stopped by and said, "Rose, I forgot to order a birthday cake, and I have no time to bake one. Can you help me?"

Rose calmed the woman and told her, "I would love to help. I will bring it by this afternoon." Rose not only baked, decorated, and delivered the cake, but she also brought Charlotte and Max over to celebrate with the child.

Telephones were a luxury that the Rozencwajgs were fortunate to own, but both customers and visitors often just showed up at their door. Rose would never turn anyone away. Every afternoon at 4 pm, she would serve tea with whatever baked good she had made earlier in the day.

*"My mother would have tea and the best cherry tart—
my favorite. And French bread with jam and coffee. We would
have a couple of neighbors come for coffee or tea, and my father
would sing songs."*

Rose was also known for her bubbeleh, a matzo meal and egg-based pancake that Jews make during Passover, when they don't eat leavened bread. The egg whites need to be whipped for quite a while to create the fluffiest bubbeleh. The whipping process was done by hand using a bulbous whisk called a "piano" whisk.

Because Passover happened in springtime, the windows of the apartments were open and the sounds of piano whisks hitting the sides of metal bowls could be heard from outside the buildings. They called this "clapping the piano." The women became very competitive and tried to outdo each other. When the bubbelehs were done, they would gather around to measure who'd made the biggest, fluffiest one, calling out in feigned surprise, "Rose, you are the winner...again!"

Rose also made homemade gefilte fish for holidays. She purchased live carp, killed the fish with a hammer, fileted them, and poached them to make the traditional dish. Rose also liked to pickle her own herring.

Charlotte enjoyed shopping with her mother in the Jewish quarter on Fridays. She had her own basket and would tell her mom to put items in it. "You can't carry all that! The basket is as big as you are!" Rose joked as Charlotte beamed with pride at being such a good helper.

When helping Rose around the house, Charlotte used a little washboard to wash handkerchiefs. She also helped her mother hang clothes inside the apartment, so they didn't have to spend money at the laundromat. After Charlotte was done with her chores, her mother usually said she could get some cherry pie from the bakery.

Rose became good friends with the baker downstairs, who also lived in their building. Even though the Rozencwajg's apartment had so many modern conveniences for the time, it only had a stovetop with a gas burner, but no oven. The baker offered the use of his oven for Rose and other women to prepare chicken dinners for Shabbat on Friday nights.

"My mother would bring a big ceramic oval dish and put a whole chicken in it with vegetables and potatoes around it and bring it to the baker. He would say, 'Come back in a couple of hours and pick it up.' There was no lid, just a pan. It's a taste you can never forget."

The chicken came out so tender that Rose would even eat the bones.

Charlotte found the practice odd. She'd cringe as her mother sat there and cracked the bones between her teeth: "Oh, mamma, stop!"

The family observed Shabbat from sundown Friday to sundown Saturday. On Sundays, they went to Mayer Shafer's kosher restaurant for dinner. His small restaurant in the 4th arrondissement was in one of Paris' most famous Jewish neighborhoods—the Marais. It was always crowded on Sunday evenings, but Mayer saved a table for his cousin's family. The food was always delicious, but Charlotte was most excited for dessert.

"They knew I liked cherry pie, and they always had the cherry pie waiting for me right there on the table if I ate my dinner. I loved sweets!"

In the fall of 1938, Mayer appeared at the Rozencwajg's apartment with an offer that stunned the couple. "We cannot stay here," he said. "I am leaving France with my family. Bring the children and come with me. We will go on a clandestine boat to the States." He was breathless as he explained his plan to Herszle and Rose.

There had been a steady rise in antisemitism in Paris, aggravated by a large influx of Jewish immigrants and the election of Léon Blum in 1936, the first Socialist and the first Jew to become prime minister. Mayer felt an urgency to leave France and go to America, and he felt an obligation to invite his cousin.

Herszle was surprised and startled at Mayer's offer. "Mayer, we don't have the money to go anywhere, much less to America."

"Don't worry about it. I will take care of everything, and you can pay me back later," Mayer insisted.

Leaving would have been a huge change for the whole family, not to mention putting them in debt. Herszle thought for a moment before giving his cousin an answer. "I came from Poland, and I learned French. Now I have to go to America and learn English?" He declined Mayer's generous offer and decided to keep his family in Paris. "Don't worry; the French are going to be good."

"My father foresaw so many things in his life; that's the only thing he didn't foresee. Mayer left and was alive after the war with his family—we didn't have that chance."

CHAPTER TWO

A Mother's Love

In 1939, as World War II erupted, Herszle joined the French army. France had military conscription as a condition of citizenship, and he was assured that after his service term ended, he would be considered a naturalized French citizen. He knew that this status would benefit his family's future. Herszle also wanted to defend his new country against any threat of invasion. He'd seen news of a surge of German troops along the French border.

Rose was anxious when Herszle left to join the army, but she knew he was doing the right thing, so she supported the decision. Plus, she didn't want to let the children see her concern. Rose worked harder to keep up with sewing jobs; without Herszle's help, it proved exceptionally difficult. She didn't want to let anyone down or turn away any of their regular clients. To balance her work with spending time with the kids, Rose often worked late into the night in order to take a break during the day to take the kids up to the terrace to play or go for a walk around the neighborhood.

Charlotte could hardly wait for her mom to say it was time to go outside. Her favorite time was playing on the terrace, but she also enjoyed walking in the neighborhood. Sometimes she would push Max in his carriage or hold her mother's hand. The trio always started their walk by passing a Catholic church across the street. "Good afternoon, Rose," the nuns called out as the three approached. Rose always stopped to chat with the nuns and their conversations ended with embraces for Rose, and a pat on the head or a pinch on the cheek for the children.

Charlotte was fascinated with the customs of the Roman Catholic Church. She enjoyed sitting in front of the window, watching the dressed-up families on Sunday mornings and holidays. She especially enjoyed when girls who were being confirmed entered the church in their white dresses and veils, looking like miniature brides. "Momma, when I am old enough, I want to dress up like that," she told Rose. Rose gently explained to her daughter that their faith did not follow that custom.

Sometimes Rose, Charlotte, and Max would take a long walk to a park between the 11th and 12th arrondissements. The park was called Place de la Nation. It was laid out in a giant circle with a roundabout for cars and lined with shops and a flower garden on the outer edge. In the center of the roundabout stood a colossal bronze statue, the Triumph of the Republic. The statue had multiple figures, including lions pulling a chariot carrying a celestial globe, upon which stood Marianne, a personification of the French Republic—liberty, equality, and fraternity. Surrounding the base of the statue was a water feature where large bronze alligators would spit water from their mouths.

"I had a little boat with a cord attached. And I would put it in the water and walk around the circle."

In the spring and summer, a carnival came to set up in Place de la Nation. There were games, vendors selling food and drinks, a carousel, and other kiddie rides. Rose often accompanied her daughter on the rides because Charlotte was too scared to ride them alone. She enjoyed them if her mother was beside her. Going to the carnival meant Charlotte would get a special treat, *pain de'epice*, a spice bread made with honey that the vendor sliced and cut into animal shapes.

"I remember when we would go to the fair. I knew I

would get pain de'epice. I loved that cookie; it was sweet, and I haven't tasted it since."

During weekdays of the school year, Rose accompanied Charlotte on the 20-minute walk to school. Most of the other parents let their children go alone. Charlotte loved school and was very upset if she missed class because of illness, which, unfortunately, was quite often. Many of her friends hated the school uniform, but Charlotte loved it—a navy blue smock with a crisp white collar.

Thursday was a day off from school and work in France, so Rose walked with the kids a short distance to the movie theater for a treat. Charlotte was a very picky eater and Rose always looked for opportunities to get her to eat. When they went to the movies, she would always pack a bag with some bread with jam and dried meat, or, another day, cheese and bread (because the family kept kosher and never mixed meat with dairy). She could always get Charlotte to eat while distracted watching her favorite American movie star, Shirley Temple. Rose made sure that she always packed extra food because, inevitably, as soon as she opened the parchment wrapping, other children in the theater would smell the homemade food and gather around her. This helped solve Rose's worries about her daughter's diet because often, when Charlotte saw her mother sharing the food with the other children, she wanted some too.

When the movie started, Charlotte could never take her eyes off the screen. She loved to watch the child actress, not much older than herself, sing and dance. She longed to be like the girl on the screen, but more than anything she wanted her beautiful curls. Charlotte's hair was fine and thin, with bangs trimmed straight across her forehead.

When they walked home from the movies, Charlotte begged her mother for curls like Shirley Temple. One afternoon, Rose gave in. "OK, Charlotte, tonight after your bath, I'm going to give you curls like Shirley Temple!"

Charlotte was so excited. She couldn't wait until her hair dried enough for her mother to use the hair curler on her. Rose heated the tongs of the hair curler over the gas burner on the stove and very carefully took a section of Charlotte's hair and began winding it around the curler. Rose was used to using the curler on herself—not on her daughter. She misjudged how close she was getting to Charlotte's head, and the hot curler touched the top of Charlotte's ear.

"Ouch!" Charlotte cried out and Rose nearly dropped the hot curler.

"Oh Lolotte, I'm so sorry!" Rose wanted to cry at the thought of hurting her daughter. That was the end of the hair curling session. The next day Rose took Charlotte to the doctor for some ointment to treat the burn.

That wasn't the only unsettling event that happened after a trip to the movie theater. There was one film in particular that frightened Charlotte so much that she couldn't shake the fear after leaving the theater. In the movie, two siblings, a brother and sister, were orphaned when their wealthy parents were killed in a plane crash. After the accident, none of the remaining family members wanted to raise the children, so they were sent to an orphanage.

Charlotte was quiet on the walk back from the movies that day, and her mother figured something other than the cold weather was bothering her daughter. When they got home, Rose placed a towel on the radiator and lifted Charlotte up to sit on it to get warm while she took off the child's shoes. While she slipped off her shoes and socks, Rose asked Charlotte how she liked the movie.

"You know, momma, I don't want you to take a trip any-where," Charlotte blurted out as fear welled up inside her. "Please don't ever take a trip because I don't want to go to an orphanage!"

In her young mind, Charlotte associated taking a trip with dying. She figured if her parents ever traveled without her and

Max, they would most certainly die and the two of them would end up in an orphanage like the siblings in the movie. She didn't know exactly what an orphanage was but given the way it was depicted in the film—as a place where children were mistreated— she knew for certain that she didn't ever want to ever go there.

"My mother squeezed me and said, 'Charlotte you are never going to go to an orphanage! First of all, I don't have the money to take a big trip. Don't worry, you never have to go to an orphanage.'"

Often, if Rose had to run an errand to one of the stores below the apartment, she would leave Charlotte and Max home alone for a short amount of time. One day, when she returned from the butcher shop, she found Charlotte dressed in one of her overcoats, with a purse over her arm and trying to keep her balance in a pair of high-heeled pumps. She was standing in her parent's bedroom in front of the armoire that had a large mirror in it, speaking what sounded like gibberish to her reflection.

Rose didn't know whether to punish her daughter for getting into her things or to laugh at the spectacle in front of her. When she asked her daughter what she was doing, Charlotte simply informed her that she was practicing her English for when she went to America.

"Are you going to leave me here when you go to America?" Rose asked.

"No, you will come with me," Charlotte told her confidently.

Rose cherished these moments that filled her often heavy heart with joy during this time when Herszle was away. She also looked forward to the weekly correspondence with her family in Poland, but the news from her first home was also getting darker.

At dawn on September 1, 1939, the German invasion of Poland began.

As the German invasion intensified across Europe, there were rumors that there would soon be bombings in Paris. Many residents fled the city to the suburbs where the thought they would be safer. Rose considered going to visit a friend in the countryside, but she didn't want to be a burden with the children.

One spring morning in 1940, there was a knock on the door. Rose opened it and was surprised to see one of the nuns, Sister Elizabeth, from the church across the street. "Rose, some of the parishioners decided that it might be best to send the children out of the city. We have a bus going shortly, and Charlotte is welcome to join us."

After Sister Elizabeth left, Rose's mind raced. She didn't want to let her daughter go, but if there was a chance for her to be safe away from the city, how could she say no? She had never lied to Charlotte before, and she wasn't quite sure if she could now. She called Charlotte into the room. "Lolotte, I was just talking to Sister Elizabeth, and they are all going to a camp in the countryside for a little while, and they want you to come too." Rose forced her voice to sound light and happy.

"Momma, I don't want to go to camp. I need to stay here and help you take care of Riri!" Rose explained that she and Max were also going away for a little while to stay with a friend. She told her daughter that this particular friend didn't have any children, so Charlotte would be bored if she came with them.

Charlotte protested some more, but soon realized she wasn't going to win the argument. As tears streamed down her cheeks, she packed some clothes in a bag and went with her mother to the front of the Église du Bon-Pasteur. Charlotte began to feel better as soon as she saw some of her friends from school getting onto the bus. No one was crying, so Charlotte wiped her face and decided to be brave.

Charlotte hugged her mother as Rose whispered in her ear, "I love you, Lolotte." Then Rose helped her up the steps of the bus. Charlotte sat by a window and waved to Rose and Max.

The bus ride was not long, and Charlotte was busy talking

with the other children. Many of them had been to summer camp before, and they liked to feel like the "knowledgeable" ones as they shared their stories with the younger children.

Since the planning for this trip was done so quickly, the nuns made use of a facility that had been vacant for a few years. When the bus pulled up to the wooden structures inside a clearing in a wooded area, the nuns hurried off the bus to try and clean up a bit so the children wouldn't be alarmed by the unkempt conditions inside the buildings.

One of the nuns came back to tell the children, "This is a more rustic camp than some of you may be used to."

Charlotte had nothing to compare it to and didn't mind the bunkhouse with rows of cots. What she didn't care for was that there was no indoor plumbing; she had to go over to a rocky area to use the bathroom. One evening, she slipped and cut her bottom on a sharp rock. The cut was quite deep, so the nuns needed to change the bandage often. She also picked up head lice from living in such close quarters with other children, and she had scratched her scalp so much that she made it bleed. The nuns thought it would be best to shave her hair and place a bandage on her scalp to help it heal.

Despite her run of bad luck, Charlotte was having fun playing the same games that she played on the terrace. The nuns made sure the children had a somewhat normal routine with scheduled meals and bedtime. Charlotte was not eating that much and liked to be one of the first ones to return her tray to the kitchen so she could go back outside to play. One afternoon, in her haste, she didn't see a banana peel that had been dropped on the wooden floor and slipped on it. When she fell, she immediately felt a sharp pain in her ankle, and when Charlotte tried to get up, she found she couldn't put any weight on it.

One of the nuns rushed over. "Oh, Charlotte dear, I think you may have broken your ankle!" Charlotte was already crying from the pain, but when she heard the nun's diagnosis, it made her cry harder.

Luckily, there was a doctor nearby who was able to come and put a cast on it. Now that Charlotte couldn't run and play outside, she just wanted to go home. She started sleeping more, partly because of the trauma to her ankle and partly because she was so sad.

A few days later, she heard, "Lolotte, Lolotte honey wake up." Charlotte thought she was dreaming when she heard her father's voice.

It wasn't a dream. "Papa!!" She wrapped her tiny arms around her father's neck and squeezed hard. "Papa, what are you doing here?"

Herszle explained that he was on furlough and heard from Rose what had happened, and wanted to come and make sure that Charlotte was all right. He could tell just by looking at the girl that she wasn't. She was bandaged, literally, from head to foot, and he tried to hide his concern about seeing his daughter in that condition. He realized that the nuns weren't really equipped to take care of so many children, but he didn't want to fault them because he knew that they cared deeply for these children. He assured the nuns that he would return to get Charlotte soon, but they told him not to worry and to get back to his battalion.

Rose and Max returned to the apartment after a brief stay outside the city. She wanted to be home, and so far, Paris seemed to be all right.

Meanwhile, Herszle couldn't get the vision of his baby girl covered in bandages out of his mind, so as soon as he could get away, he went back to the camp, picked up Charlotte, and took her home.

Shortly after Rose and Charlotte's return to Paris, things began to change. On the morning of June 14, 1940, Parisians awoke to the sound of a stern voice, in an unfamiliar German accent, announcing via loudspeakers across the city that a curfew was being imposed starting at 8 pm that evening. Germany had invaded. The city known so famously for its light, grew dark and somber.

Rose and the children stayed in the apartment most days, as the appearance of military vehicles and German soldiers in the city made Rose apprehensive to venture too far from home. When they went up to the terrace, many parents now accompanied the children, and they would share their fears about what was happening and whether they should leave Paris. Rose thought about leaving, too, but didn't want to make such a decision alone, and she missed her husband dearly.

Herszle came home to his family near the end of 1940. A bullet to his upper thigh brought his service days to an early end. Although he would fully recover, France did not hold up its end of the deal on granting him naturalization.

While in the service, Herszle became close friends with his general, Maurice Vinciguerra. When the war ended, the general went on to law school and became an attorney. The men remained good friends, and years after the war, the general took on Herszle's case against France and was able to successfully get him his citizenship granted.

Armed German soldiers were now a common sight on the streets of Paris. Everyone spokes in hushed tones. The Germans went door to door, inquiring as to who was Jewish and instructing those residents to go to a specific address so that they could register with the "authorities."

Herszle was not so quick to follow their orders, but Rose begged her husband to do as they instructed. "Please, Herszle, I don't want any trouble."

"OK, my Róza, but I am not doing it for them; I am doing it for you," he consoled her, using his pet name for her. He agreed to go, but only if he could go alone. He wasn't sure what was going to happen when he went to register, and he would feel better if his family was safe at home.

When Herszle arrived at the registration location, he recognized many of the Jews from his building waiting in line. He felt the tension in the air as each approached the table manned by a

German soldier and gave their name. When it was Herszle's turn, he told them his name, and he was given paperwork with a stamp on it that said *Juif* (Jew in French). He was instructed to carry the papers with him at all times for identification purposes. He then was told to wait in another line. When he got to the front of that line, he was asked how many members were in the family, and the officer behind the table proceeded to give him a stack of yellow pieces of fabric with the Star of David printed on them with the word *Juif* written in the middle in bold, black lettering. He was instructed that anyone age six and over would have to wear the star on their clothing, on the left side of the chest, whenever they left the house.

Herszle returned home with an uneasy feeling, unable to completely process what he just experienced. It didn't take long for his shock and surprise to turn to indignation. He took out his needle and thread and began stitching the yellow star onto the lapel of his overcoat. He went to his sewing table and retrieved a bit of cotton batting, which he inserted underneath the star. If the Germans wanted to know who Jewish was, then he would make sure his star stood out!

When Charlotte returned to school, the teachers were all instructed to make the Jewish children sit in the back of the class. This did not go over well with the first-grade teacher, whose favorite student was Charlotte. Sometimes she would take her for cherry pie after school, and one time, she even made Charlotte walk around the classroom with her work pinned on her back to show the other children what a well-done assignment looked like. Her teacher was so proud of her, as she knew that Charlotte did not speak French at home and that the girl was doing all the work alone, without help from her parents.

The teacher knew what a dedicated student Charlotte was and that she always liked to sit in the front of the class. Now she was supposed to put her and the other Jewish children in the back and ignore them.

When Charlotte walked in that morning she first wore the

yellow star, the teacher motioned her over. "Here, Charlotte," she said as she tied a scarf across her chest to hide the yellow star, "go ahead and sit up front." Then she nodded, assuring Charlotte it would be all right.

"The teacher told the students that anyone who made fun of Jewish kids, I wasn't the only one, would be severely punished. They weren't even allowed to play with us in the schoolyard. But the teacher said that it was OK to play with us, and as long as she said it was OK, no one could say it wasn't."

Some of the Jewish children stopped going to school. The ones that were left would walk home together, and more parents than usual seemed to be walking their children home from school in those days. While they were walking, if a German soldier was coming toward them, they all had to move off the sidewalk onto the gutter and walk in the street with the oncoming cars. Everywhere Charlotte went in Paris, she could feel tension. The antisemitism was getting worse.

"They took away the movies, the theaters, there was no more entertainment for us. If we took the subway or the train, we had to ride in the last car. If there was a food line, we had to wait at the end. It seemed like we were always at the end of the line because we could never get to the front. Whenever they saw a Jew get close to the front of the line, they made them get back."

Even in their own apartment building, things were changing. One day Charlotte was up on the terrace playing a game with her friends where they were making up funny nicknames for each other based on the names of vegetables. When it got to be Charlotte's turn, she turned to her friend, an Italian boy, and blurted out "macaroni." She wasn't sure if it was a vegetable or not, but it was the first thing that came to mind. Charlotte had no idea that the term "macaroni" was a derogatory term to Italians, and the boy went home and told his father because his feelings were hurt.

Later that evening, there was a loud pounding on the Rozencwajg's door. Herszle answered it and found a very upset man who pointed at Charlotte and said, "She disrespected my son today!"
Charlotte felt her face flush as she recognized the man as the Italian boy's father.

"You dirty Jews," he said, "don't you ever call me or my son macaroni!" As he left, he slammed the door behind him.

Even though she was young, Charlotte began to understand that things weren't the same as they used to be and seemed to be getting worse. Worry took a toll on her health. Already a sickly child, Rose was used to taking Charlotte to the doctor or clinic. She'd had whooping cough, scarlet fever, and often, an upset stomach.

When Charlotte was five years old, her appendix burst. She woke up in the middle of the night screaming in pain. The ambulance came and rushed her to the hospital, where they performed emergency surgery to save her life. After her surgery, she spent a week in a convalescent home in Dreux, about 45 miles from Paris.

This particular morning, Charlotte was in an upbeat mood. She was positioned in her favorite spot, watching the comings and goings on the street through the large picture window. The sun's warmth from the morning light felt good on her face and she was gazing lazily down the street when she realized what she was looking at was not normal.

Several trucks were parked about a half a block down the street. German soldiers and French police officers were ushering men into the backs of the trucks. Other men lined up on the sidewalk. In their hands were suitcases. She called out to her father, "Papa, come quick! I don't know what's happening, but they are putting people in trucks!"

CHAPTER THREE

In Hiding

Herszle knew immediately that something was wrong. He looked out the window with Charlotte but didn't know what to make of the scene that was unfolding on the street below. He decided to go downstairs to find out, but he assured Charlotte not to worry because, after all, he had been a soldier in the French army, so surely, he would have some protection because of that.

He had a special order to be delivered to an address just past where the trucks were parked, so Herszle figured he could walk by with his package tucked under his arm and try to catch a glimpse of what was going on without drawing too much attention to himself. As he walked past, one of the gendarmes pulled on his arm and forced Herszle to stop.

"Identification!" said the officer sharply.

Herszle got a bad feeling in the pit of his stomach as he handed over his papers with the Jewish stamp on them. The gendarme glanced at the paperwork, folded it in half, and handed it back to Herszle.

"OK, stand over there," the man instructed Herszle to stand with the others lined up on the sidewalk.

Instead of doing as instructed, Herszle started to walk back toward the apartment. The gendarme called out to him to stop, but he just started walking faster. When Herszle reached the steps of the apartment building, the officer had caught up with him. Thinking quickly, Herszle explained that he wasn't who they were looking for but that the "right man" was inside the apartment. Herszle opened the door and gestured for the police officer to go in ahead of him. But just as the officer crossed the threshold, Herszle said, "There's the man you are looking for!" and shoved the policeman into the apartment and slammed the door.

Rose, startled by the commotion, turned the corner to see a gendarme in her living room with a very surprised look on his face.

"Where is your husband?" the officer shouted at her. She was so scared that the police were in her home, looking for her husband, that she could barely get out the words, "I don't know."

Disgusted, and embarrassed that he had let Herszle get away, the officer turned and left the apartment.

Meanwhile, Herszle had taken the stairs two at a time up to the third-floor apartment of Madame Roland. Luckily, she answered his knock, saw he was breathless, and ushered him inside. He explained to her what was happening in the street below and his own encounter with the gendarme. She told him to sit down and calm himself until they could figure out what to do next.

In the meantime, Rose was in a panic. When evening came, she was startled by a knock on the door and heard, "Rose, let me in." It was Madame Roland, who explained that Herszle was safe in her apartment, but he needed a suitcase with a few toiletries and some clothing. She told Rose that it would be too dangerous for him to stay in the building, since the officers would be on the lookout for him. She had contacted an acquaintance who agreed that Herszle could stay with him for a while.

"Rose, Herszle also told me to tell you to put all your valuables in the duvet cover. I will put them in my closet for safe keeping," said Madame Roland.

Rose looked at the woman with bewilderment, but she trusted Madame Roland and she knew her husband must have a good reason for her to do such an odd thing.

Rose went to work, removing the white zippered coverlet from the bed, and began retrieving items from her jewelry box and snapshots stashed in drawers and framed photos hanging on the wall. She also went to the secret drawer in the back of the armoire and took out some of their most valuable possessions. Charlotte and Max had been watching quietly, and Charlotte knew by the tone of the two women talking and the way that her mother was moving erratically through the apartment that something was going on.

"Lolotte, I'm going to put your ring in here, the one with your initials on it," said Rose.

The ring had come from Herszle's mother in Poland when Charlotte was two years old. It was gold with a flat top where the initials "LR" were inscribed in script lettering. Those initials stood for Leah Rozencwajg, Charlotte's Hebrew name.

In fact, when the ring first arrived in the mail, Herszle placed it in Charlotte's tiny hand, and not knowing the sentiment or the value of the object, she threw it on the floor and stepped on it. She then picked it up and threw it out the window. Herszle ran downstairs and retrieved it. Charlotte was just too little at the time to realize what a treasured possession it truly was. Ever since then, it had been stored in the secret drawer of the armoire.

"My father retrieved it because it came from his mother. That ring I can never forget. I never saw my grandparents or met them."

When Rose was finished, she handed her neighbor her most cherished possessions inside the duvet cover.

"May I come up to your apartment and see Herszle?" she asked Madame Roland.

"Herszle thought it best if you don't. He figured that someone is probably watching to see if you leave the apartment. He said to tell you and the children that he loves you very much."

Fighting back tears, Madame Roland told Rose that he was

able to contact the people who offered to hide him, and he would be leaving as soon as it got dark.

Rose had been on her own with the children before, when Herszle was in the army, but this time felt different. She felt lonely and fearful. Things seemed to get worse by the day. The Germans were completely running Paris, and supplies grew scarcer as the prices got higher. Rose had lost almost all her tailoring clients, which was probably good because she couldn't get fabric most of the time anyway. She couldn't even listen to the radio as all it contained was German propaganda. She heard from Herszle sporadically; he had already moved several times because not everyone wanted to hide a Jew.

In the beginning of the summer of 1942, a gendarme who patrolled the neighborhood came to the Rozencwajg's door. "Good morning, Rose. I need to tell you something. Can we talk?" Rose walked into the hallway and closed the apartment door behind her. Her heart hammered wildly in her chest as she thought that something had happened to Herszle.

"The Germans are planning to pick up the women and children tomorrow, so if you have a place to hide, please do so."

Rose didn't even get to say a word, and the officer was gone. Hide? Where would she and the children hide? Her mind raced. Panic set in.

She had heard from Herszle the day before. He sent an address where he could receive telegrams. Rose decided to send a telegram to her husband to ask what he thought she should do. It didn't take long for her to get a response: "Go to Sister Elizabeth – (stop) – second choice Madame Peron – (stop) – all my love, Herszle – (stop)."

Rose felt a sense of relief knowing that she now had a plan. She would ask the nuns at Église du Bon-Pasteur if they could hide at the church. When Max went down for a nap that afternoon, Rose told Charlotte she was running an errand and went over to the church.

Sister Elizabeth greeted Rose when she knocked on the back door of the church. "Rose, what a pleasant surprise!" The nun embraced Rose and invited her inside.

"Sister, I have been told that the Germans are picking up the Jewish woman and children tomorrow, and we are in need of a place to hide." Saying it out loud made Rose feel ill.

The nun hadn't heard this news, but she was not surprised. "Rose, I'm afraid we don't have the room to hide all three of you; our quarters are quite small. I can offer to hide Charlotte—would that be of help?"

"Yes, I completely understand; thank you, Sister. I will bring Charlotte over this evening."

As Rose walked back across the street, she decided to take a detour and see if she could catch Charlotte's nursery school teacher and the director of the preschool, Mademoiselle Peron. The nursery school was just a 10-minute walk from their apartment, and Mademoiselle Peron was still there when Rose arrived.

"Rose is everything all right?" the director asked when she saw her.

"Actually, no," Rose replied, and she went on to relay the same information she'd told to Sister Elizabeth. Mademoiselle Peron was shocked but assured her that they could stay in the room above the school that was currently empty. Rose hugged the woman, thanked her profusely, and then hastily headed back home to pack.

When Rose arrived back at the apartment, Charlotte could tell something was wrong by the look on her mother's face. "Momma, what is it? What's wrong?"

Rose sat down on the floor with her daughter and took both of her hands in hers. "Lolotte, remember how the Germans were looking for Papa and he had to hide from them?" Rose looked deep into Charlotte's eyes. Charlotte nodded as her mother continued, "Tomorrow, they are looking for the women and children, so we must hide."

Rose explained that Charlotte would hide with the nuns, and Rose would take Max to the nursery school. She stressed that this was a temporary situation until Herszle could come up with a plan where they could all be together again.

Charlotte was scared but knew that she must be brave. She got her small suitcase and packed it with some of her clothes and her spool dolls. Rose decided it would be best to leave when it was dark. She didn't know what time the Germans would come around in the morning, and she didn't want to take any chances.

After dinner, Rose, Max, and Charlotte held hands and walked across the street to the Catholic church. Charlotte usually looked forward to walks, but tonight her chest felt heavy, and her legs felt like lead as they walked. Sister Elizabeth was waiting in the dark in the back garden, and she and Rose talked in hushed tones.

Rose gave Charlotte a big hug and kissed her on the cheek. "I love you, Lolotte," her voice cracked with emotion as she said goodbye. Charlotte was trying to be brave, but the tears came anyway.

"I love you, momma." She didn't want to let go, but Max was getting impatient and was pulling on Rose's skirt. "I love you too, Riri," said Charlotte as she hugged Max and kissed him on top of the head.

"Come on, Charlotte," said Sister Elizabeth, trying to sound upbeat as she, too, was fighting back emotion. "Let's get you settled."

Charlotte would be staying in Sister Elizabeth's room, and she had made the girl a small bed in the corner with some pillows and blankets. She showed Charlotte the bathroom and told her that she couldn't go outside in the garden unless there was someone with her, and she could never go out front.

"I understand," Charlotte said.

Several days later, Sister Elizabeth was on her morning walk when she saw a printed sign with a swastika on it on the fencepost. The sign was a warning to anyone helping or hiding Jews.

It stated that if you helped a Jew, you would be treated as if you were Jewish and would meet with the appropriate punishment.

Sister Elizabeth hurried back to the church and shared what she had seen with the other nuns. They all agreed that they could not put themselves or their parishioners in peril. Charlotte could not stay there any longer.

Charlotte was playing quietly in her corner of the room when Sister Elizabeth entered.

"Charlotte, I'm so sorry, but you can't stay here any longer," the nun said as tears rolled down her cheeks. "I'm going to take you to the nursery school to be with your mom."

> *"It was amazing that there were a lot of nice people we knew. The nursery was 10 minutes from our apartment. The whole neighborhood knew us. It was unbelievable that no matter where we went, we were a step ahead and knew that we had to move. There were good people and bad people. In today's life, it is the same way."*

At first, Charlotte was fearful hearing the nun's words, but when she said that she would take her to her mom and Max, she became excited. She gathered up her belongings and was ready to go.

It was a short walk from the church to the nursery school, and Charlotte kept her head down. Sister Elizabeth told her to take off her yellow star for the time being and figured if she were asked any questions, she would say she was taking an orphan to a possible home.

> *"We kept the Jewish star on. We were in hiding, but we didn't realize we should take the star off."*

When they arrived at the preschool, Mademoiselle Peron greeted them. She knew Sister Elizabeth and that Charlotte had been hiding at the church. She could tell by looking at the nun's face the pain she felt at not being able to keep Charlotte, but she had also seen the signs the Germans posted and understood. Mademoiselle Peron was petrified, too, but she loved Charlotte and her family and felt she had to do everything she could to help.

Mademoiselle Peron embraced Charlotte and said, "Come." She took the tiny child's hand in her own and guided her up the narrow stairwell. She opened the door at the top of the stairs, and Rose was seated on the floor with Max on her lap.

"Momma! Riri!" Charlotte ran to embrace her mother and brother.

"We were the only people hiding in the nursery. It was sad. My mother didn't know what was going to happen, so she always kept us very tight. She felt that, somehow, we would be separated. It was at that time she would always say, 'Look out for your brother; try to keep an eye out for your brother if anything happens to me.' "I would always say, 'Nothing is going to happen. I am always going with you wherever you're going to go.'"

A couple of other people who worked at the nursery school knew that the trio was hiding upstairs. They brought math and spelling worksheets for Charlotte to keep her occupied. They gave Max some blocks and a toy truck. One woman employee also sewed, and brought up some fabric, needles, and thread for Rose.

The three of them stayed in that single room day after day. The preschool let new teachers stay in that small apartment until they found their own place near the school. The room had a twin bed and a table with four chairs. There was also a bathroom, so there was no need for them to ever venture downstairs.

Mademoiselle Peron brought up breakfast one morning and motioned Rose over to the corner of the room. "Rose, members of the Gestapo have been coming by and asking questions. I'm afraid they will want to search the building," she glanced down at the floor as she finished her sentence.

Rose took the teachers hands in her own. "You have done so much for us; I don't want anything to happen to you or anyone here," she tried to hide the fear in her voice. "I will get ahold of Herszle and see where he is and if we can join him."

Mademoiselle Peron hugged Rose tight, "I'm so sorry."

Herszle had been constantly on the move, hiding with whoever would take him in for any length of time. He heard that Jews were traveling to Vichy into the so-called *zone libre* (free zone) that the Nazis had not yet occupied. Initially, Herszle wanted to take his family to Switzerland, but when he investigated that option, he discovered that it would be far too expensive for them to all travel there.

In the last place he'd been hiding, he made a connection with a man who was arranging for families to be transported to Vichy. Herszle asked them to put him in touch with this person.

In the meantime, he received a telegram from Rose about what was going on at the nursery and that they would have to leave very soon.

The next day, Herszle met the man. He told Herszle how much it would cost to get the family to Vichy. "I will take you and your wife first and then send for the children. In the meantime, I have made arrangements for them to stay at the orphanage on Rue Lamarck."

Since Herszle did not have that much cash, the man also agreed to take jewelry as payment. The man was a fellow Jew, and Herszle felt that he could trust him to help get his family out of Paris. Under the cover of darkness, he returned to Madame Roland's to retrieve some valuables from the duvet cover to use as payment.

He contacted Rose and told her of the plan. She was so relieved that the whole family would be able to escape Paris and go to Vichy. She wasn't sure what would happen once they got there, but she had gotten used to making plans minute-by-minute, and all that mattered was having Herszle by her side and keeping her children safe.

The plan was to drop the children off a couple of days before they left to avoid arousing suspicion with the authorities by having a large group drop off children all on the same day.

As Charlotte rode the metro with her mother and Max, her stomach was unsettled. She knew the plan, but in her mind, she kept thinking of the movie where the children went to the orphanage and how awful it was. After getting off the metro, they headed down the Rue Lamarck, with the view of Sacré-Coeur Basilica in the distance.

Arriving at the orphanage, Rose entered with the children. A tall, thin woman with her hair piled high in a bun, Madame Becotte welcomed them. When Rose told them her name, Madame Becotte said that she had been expecting them. She first showed Charlotte the dormitory that she would be sleeping in. It was a large room with rows of beds. The woman pointed to where Charlotte could place her things in a small trunk beside the bed.

Max would be staying in another room with younger children, she explained. Max had been acting fussy all day, but Rose just thought it was all the changes going on. The woman assured her that her children would be well taken care of and not to worry.

The next day at breakfast, Madame Becotte approached Charlotte. "Charlotte, your brother was taken to the hospital late last night. He developed a rash and a high fever." She explained that the doctors thought it was scarlet fever and he would have to stay in the hospital for a while.

Charlotte was worried about Max and hoped that he wasn't scared all alone in the hospital. Some of the children saw that she was upset and invited her to play dolls with them. So far, the orphanage was nothing like it was in the movie, but Charlotte was still glad that she had both a mom and a dad and would not have to stay there very long.

The day her parents were headed to Vichy, they both came to

say goodbye. Max was still in the hospital, and Rose and Herszle debated whether to say goodbye to him first or Charlotte. They figured that they would have to pass by the hospital on the way out of town, so they could stop by and see Charlotte first.

Charlotte was sad to see her mother and father go, but her parents reassured her that they would be together soon. Herszle kissed his daughter, hugged her tight, and told Rose he would be waiting outside. Charlotte was so close to her mom; most days, her mother still dressed her and fed her. Charlotte asked her mother how she would be able to take care of herself.

"Lolotte, I will ask one of the nice ladies who work here to take extra care of you," then she looked her daughter in the eye as her tone got more serious. "Listen, Lolotte, if anything happens to me, rely on Madame Roland and Madame Elazare. You can always find a person who will send a telegram for you. Also, watch out for Riri. He needs you."

Charlotte nodded and recited her address out loud to her mother, "166 Rue de Charonne," she had memorized it at a young age, and her mother smiled, fighting back tears as she gathered her daughter in her arms and held her tight.

Everyone saying goodbye had assembled in the large dining hall. There were 30 other Jewish children who would be staying temporarily at the orphanage. The room had been silent as families talked in hushed tones with the occasional sound of some sniffling and soft crying.

Then, the mood in the room changed in an instant. The side doors burst open, and several armed German police barged into the room. The quiet was broken by screams of terror as the soldiers grabbed the adults and forced them outside. The children were instructed to stay back and out of the way.

Charlotte saw a pregnant woman try to hide by crawling under one of the long tables and a soldier ran up, and grabbing her by the hair, dragged her out from under the table as she kicked and screamed. There was another woman clutching a tiny infant, and the Gestapo officer ripped the baby from her arms.

As the mother looked on in horror, he threw the infant into the air as if it was a toy, and as the mother lurched forward in an attempt to catch her child, the baby hit the floor with a horrific sound and went motionless.

Charlotte looked around the room in a panic as she saw an officer forcing her mother through the door to the outside. She went to run towards the open doors but was intercepted and held tight. Charlotte heard Madame Becotte's voice in her ear, "Charlotte, you can't go with them. You have to stay here."

CHAPTER FOUR

The Romanian, the Janitor, and the Madame

It was August 1942.

"When they took away my mom, it was like cutting my arm or leg off. I was always taken care of. She was feeding me, even at 10 years old, and she was dressing me. So, when they took her away, I felt it was the end of the world coming."

Inside the orphanage, tension and fear hung thick in the air. Some of the children had run to hide when the Germans were dragging their parents out, while others just stood transfixed in a state of shock, afraid that if they moved, they would wake up from this nightmare and it would all become real.

Staff members at the orphanage were just as stunned at the situation as it unfolded. The Germans had told them that they would only be watching the children for a few weeks until they could be sent off to join their parents in Vichy. They were expecting some tears from the children as they said goodbye to their parents, and were prepared to console them for this brief time with the assurance that they would soon be reunited. Now, as they looked around, all they saw were traumatized children. The halls of the orphanage were filled with the sounds of their inconsolable wailings.

The caretakers were overwhelmed by the 30 hysterical children, in addition to the more than 40 they'd taken in before. Charlotte wasn't sure who it was that her mother had spoken to; who had agreed to take care of her? The staff desperately tried to engage the children with games or songs, but they weren't having much luck. To make matters worse, none of them knew any of the familiar Jewish songs that their parents had sung to comfort them when they were afraid.

Charlotte wasn't hysterical because she was still trying to piece together everything that had happened. She was thankful that her brother wasn't there to witness the horror. She speculated that if her parents had chosen to visit Max in the hospital instead of coming to see her first, they might have been able to see the Germans arrive at the orphanage. Perhaps they could've avoided capture.

That evening, Charlotte was surprised when she was told she had a visitor. When she walked down the stairs, she was elated to see a familiar face. It was her father! She ran down the rest of the steps and leaped into his arms. Because she was unsure about ever seeing either of her parents again, Charlotte felt a small flame of hope ignite within her when she saw her father.

Charlotte stared at her father in disbelief. Her mind raced to thoughts of where her mother was and whether she was alright. Sensing his daughter's concern, Herszle said what he could to reassure her. "Charlotte don't worry. I will do whatever I can to get you out of here."

As much as it pained him, Herszle knew he could not stay in any one place for very long and he told Charlotte that he had to leave but that he would be back as soon as he could. He gave her a long hug and a kiss on the forehead, and then he was gone again.

Herszle left the orphanage thinking about how quickly his life had changed in the span of 10 hours. A lump formed in his throat as he remembered the events that had unfolded around the capture. As Rose was forced outside the orphanage, she and Herszle reunited as the German soldiers ordered all the parents at gunpoint into the back of military vehicles. The large grey trucks had open beds, and when all the people had been loaded onto a vehicle, an armed officer jumped in to oversee the human cargo. As the trucks started pulling away from the orphanage, Herszle realized that there was no armed officer in the back of their truck, and they were the last ones in the convoy.

He had a bad feeling about where they were headed, so he devised a plan. He whispered to Rose that they were about to enter a very narrow street where the driver would be forced to slow down and that they should try to escape by jumping off the back of the truck.

The idea terrified Rose. "No, Herszle. I can't. If I jump, they are going to find me and kill me. I won't see the kids again." Her voice broke as she fought back tears.

Herszle took her hands in his and stared deep into her eyes as he pleaded with his wife, "We only live once. Róza, please."
When the truck entered the narrow street, Herszle decided to act.

He jumped.

When he landed, he realized Rose was not beside him.

He turned to look at the truck as the distance grew between him and the love of his life. He wanted to yell out her name but couldn't risk bringing attention to himself. Instead, he just stared at his wife's beautiful face until the truck rounded a corner and was gone.

For days, Charlotte felt numb. She couldn't grasp the enormity of the situation as she walked the halls. All she could think about was how much her life had been turned upside down in such a short period of time. The children tried to comfort each other. A few helped Charlotte pick out and put on her clothing in the morning. It was a simple activity, yet it was something she never had to do for herself.

"We were sleeping in a dormitory in the orphanage. I had a good friend named Helen. I was crying in bed because my mother was gone. Helen was holding my hand. She told me, 'Don't cry...don't cry...things are going to get better.'"

It felt so strange for Charlotte to be in an environment where all the children were Jewish, but none of the adults were. The caretakers tried to make the kids as comfortable as possible, but many children were always crying and asking for their parents. One day, after Charlotte had been there about two weeks, the director of the orphanage called the children downstairs. She made them all gather in a group at the foot of the staircase. Charlotte was small, so she ended up in front.

A woman appeared with another employee. Madame Becotte motioned towards the children and said, "Pick whomever you want."

The director was exhausted. She knew that the parents of these children were never coming back. She figured the best thing for them would be to see that they were adopted so they could start new lives.

The woman scanned the group of children. Her eyes settled on Charlotte. "I'll take her," the woman said. She had a thick Romanian accent.

"She took me to her apartment near the Eiffel Tower. When I arrived at her place she said, 'Charlotte it's the war, and we don't have much food, so you are going to have an apple and a piece of bread for the day. And we can't afford to bathe. You don't need to bathe. But when you get to that castle where I'm sending you, you are going to get everything you want.'"

The apartment wasn't as modern as the Rozencwajg's former home, but there was an indoor toilet and sink that Charlotte had access to. This woman lived with her parents and a baby. There was no sign of a husband, and Charlotte wondered if he might have joined the war to fight or if he had been taken by the Germans. She had no idea if this family was Jewish.

The woman left early in the morning for work and didn't return until almost dark, leaving the girl in the care of the baby's grandparents, who barely acknowledged her presence. The only time she interacted with them was in the afternoon when the grandmother placed the infant in a baby carriage and told Charlotte they were going to the park. She told her to bring her apple and slice of bread so she could have a "picnic."

The three would then walk to the Champs de Mars. As she walked, Charlotte thought of happier times when her family had come to the park at the base of the Eiffel Tower. It seemed odd that she was now here at such a familiar place with a stranger. Would she ever get her old life back again?

Charlotte sat in the grass and ate her meager rations while the grandmother ate her lunch, which was far more substantial than Charlotte's. She had noticed that although the Romanian woman had told her that food was limited, the family always seemed to eat quite well during their mealtimes. They never offered Charlotte anything more than bread and an apple.

When Charlotte returned to the apartment building, she knew that the grandparents wouldn't be watching her. She liked to sneak out and visit the lady janitor who took care of the building's maintenance needs. Even though Charlotte was just 10 years old, she was a very social child, and she missed her former lifestyle in the other apartment, where she often visited with neighbors and friends.

The janitor was a kind woman. She would always have a treat, like cookies or candy, when Charlotte came to visit because she looked forward to talking with the little girl. Many of the residents in the building paid little attention to her except when they needed something. Seeing Charlotte brightened her day.

During a visit one afternoon, the janitor surprised Charlotte by saying, "You know, Charlotte, I would like to know what happens in that apartment. All the children the woman has brought to live there have disappeared."

It didn't take Charlotte long to figure out the answer.

One night, quite a while after dark, there was a knock on the door. As the Romanian woman answered, Charlotte was playing quietly in a corner of the dining room. The girl couldn't see the man who knocked on the door, but she overheard the conversation. They were speaking German and even though she didn't know the language, Charlotte realized she could understand this particular dialect because it was similar to her native Yiddish.

She heard the woman say, "When are you going to give me the money for her?"

The man replied, "When I pick her up, I will give you the money."

The Romanian woman asked him to give her a couple more days.

Charlotte held in a gasp when she realized that they were talking about her, but she kept on playing so that they would not suspect she had understood.

The next morning, Charlotte found the janitor and told her about the conversation. "I think I'm going away someplace, but I think it's not a good place because it's with the Germans."

"Is there anyone who we can contact who could come pick you up?" the janitor asked. The question made Charlotte remember the last conversation she'd had with her mother at the orphanage.

She told the janitor that she had to get a telegram to Madame Roland, and she recited the address to her former apartment building because her mother had made her memorize it "in case of an emergency." She hoped that since Madame Roland was not Jewish, she would still be at home.

The janitor promised to get a telegram off right away, and Charlotte returned to the apartment so as not to raise any suspicion.

At 6 pm that evening, there was a knock on the door. Charlotte froze for a minute, wondering if it was the German again. Were they coming to take her away early? The Romanian woman answered the door and Charlotte heard a familiar voice asking to see the girl. It was Madame Elazare, her best friend Betty's mom. When Madame Roland had received the telegram, she immediately went to Madame Elazare's apartment. Madame Roland was afraid to go pick Charlotte up, so Madame Elazare agreed to do it.

Charlotte overheard the Romanian woman say, "What are you doing here? Who told you that she was here?"

The rescuer calmly explained that Charlotte's mother had told her that she was at the orphanage and when she went there, they told her that Charlotte had been adopted by the people who lived at that address. Charlotte felt a wave of relief that the janitor would never be suspected as being the one who'd provided the information.

"I just want to see her. Maybe take her for a little walk, just for a little while."

The Romanian woman objected. "But we were just getting ready to have supper."

Charlotte mumbled to herself that her "supper," an apple and a piece of bread, had been eaten hours earlier.

"Don't worry, I'll bring her back in time for supper," Madame Elazare assured the woman.

The Romanian woman consented. She let Charlotte go with Madame Elazare and as the two were walking down the front steps, she called out, "Have her back soon!"

Charlotte wanted to run away from that place as fast as she could, but Madame Elazare held her hand tightly as they walked away from the apartment building. Charlotte looked back and saw the janitor in the window waving at her. She dared not wave back in case the Romanian woman was looking out the window, but she flashed her a big smile.

They walked quickly to the closest metro station to board the subway for the half-hour ride home. Once on the subway,

Madame Elazare turned to take a good look at Charlotte. She barely recognized the girl. The skin on her arms and legs was black from the filth in the apartment and not being able to bathe. Her long hair was knotted, matted, and covered with lice. And then there was the stench.

When they reached the place where Charlotte had spent her earlier years, Madame Elazare placed her in the tub and scrubbed Charlotte's skin for what seemed like hours. She then had to cut her hair short because it was in such bad shape that she couldn't get a comb through it. Madame Elazare found a dress made from fabric scraps for Charlotte to wear, and when she was done cleaning her up, she was so proud of how she had transformed the girl that she took a photo of Charlotte standing next to Betty.

Although Charlotte was happy to see her best friend and be safely away from the Romanian woman, she was sad to be so close to her former apartment and not be able to go home. Madame Elazare made some clothes for her from scraps of fabric (her sewing abilities were nothing like Herszle's and Rose's). Charlotte slept in a crib in a corner of Betty's room. Charlotte thought it odd that they still had a crib up since Betty was 11 and an only child, but Charlotte was so tiny that she was able to sleep in it comfortably.

Charlotte didn't recognize most of the faces who greeted her in the hallways. The Germans had not started picking up the French Jews yet, but since so many of the residents were Jewish, many of the families left out of fear. Madame Elazare was constantly worried about when the Germans would come for her family. She had always been strict with Betty; even before the war, she would never let her go up to play on the terrace. Now she never let the girl out of her sight. The Elazare's apartment was more expensive than Charlotte's, and it had a private balcony that overlooked the center courtyard. The girls were allowed out there to play, but Madame Elazare didn't allow them to leave the building to take a walk or go to the park. When the girls played outside, Charlotte often looked up wistfully to the now-empty playground. She had so many fond memories of playing up there. Mr. Elazare, a kind and soft-spoken man, tried to convince his wife to let the girls at least go to the park, but he never won that argument.

Madame Elazare was also concerned about the German occupation, but, like most people, she was mostly unaware of the atrocities that were taking place. Even though she believed that the people who had left were at work camps, she did not want to have to leave her home and Betty behind.

A new neighbor Madame Elazare befriended would come over for afternoon tea. One day she told Madame Elazare that she'd come up with a solution to her constant worrying about the Germans coming to pick them up. "You know, Ilene," she said, "if you convert to Christian Science, like me, then you won't have to say you are Jewish. You won't have to worry." That was all the prompting that Madame Elazare needed, and despite her husband's objections, she was attending the Christian Science church with Betty and Charlotte in tow the next week.

In the night, Charlotte would awaken and hope that her father would come pick her up soon. It had been months since she'd seen him in the orphanage. Although Madame Elazare had assured Charlotte she could stay with them as long as she needed to, and although Charlotte was grateful for what Madame Elazare had done to rescue her from the Romanian woman, she missed her own family and wanted to be with them.

Years later, Charlotte learned how truly lucky she was that she had been "adopted" by the Romanian woman. That experience had saved her life. It was while she was with the Romanians, and while her brother was still in the hospital, that the Germans raided the orphanage. They deported the 79 resident Jewish children to Auschwitz. Of that number, 71 of them, including Helen who comforted Charlotte, were murdered at the concentration camp.

CHAPTER FIVE

Herszle's Plan

Madame Ilene Elazare received a telegram from Herszle one morning. In it, he asked, "Do you know where Charlotte is?"

She sent one back in reply: "Yes, she's here with me. But I don't know how much longer I can keep her."

Despite the Elazares' conversion to Christian Science to keep a low profile, Charlotte still maintained her Jewish identity. No one knew how long it would be before it was no longer safe for the girl. Madame Elazare had watched many of the people around her be taken to work camps, and she, like everyone else, did not have any idea of the atrocities that were happening to them. In fact, several of her friends had gone willfully to the camps, thinking that if they offered to go with a friend, they would at least know someone when they got there.

Ilene recalled a conversation she'd once had with Herszle when they lived as neighbors. He'd told her his intuition was telling him that many of the places people were being sent to weren't just "work" camps. He seemed to know something more.

After the telegram exchange, Herszle contacted Madame Elazare and explained that he was currently in the Ardennes, in a village called Beaumont-en-Argonne. It was a place where, in May 1940, the Germans came through France when they'd taken over Belgium and the Netherlands. At that time, the German army used the combined force of tanks, mobile infantry, and artillery troops to drive through the Ardennes Forest and penetrate the Allied defenses.

The small, close-knit village where everyone called each other "cousin" in the north of France had now been taken over by the Germans as a strategic point due to its proximity to the German border. The cobblestoned streets of Beaumont-en-Argonne were laid out like a chessboard; the Church of St. John the Baptist (Église Saint-Jean-Baptiste) and the mayor's building were located on the main square. A Schutzstaffel (SS) officer named Faust was put in charge of the town, and he set up operations in a home across the street from the post office.

Included as part of the occupation of that village, the Germans took over surrounding farmland to establish the agricultural operations that fed their troops. Needing free labor to work the land, they brought in Jews from other parts of France to work the fields. Herszle was told that, as long as he willingly agreed to come there to work, he would not be deported out of France. He was assured that his wife would also not be deported, although no one would tell him her current location.

He did not know that after they were separated in Paris, his beloved Rose was sent to Drancy, an internment camp in a northeastern suburb of Paris. In the summer of 1942, Drancy became a major transit camp for the deportation of Jews. From Drancy, Rose boarded a train to her ultimate destination in the Polish countryside—Auschwitz.

Herszle grew tired of constantly being on the run. Shortly after he visited Charlotte in the orphanage, he was approached by some gendarmes who asked him for identification. He paused for a moment, acting as if he was getting out his wallet, and as he did, he turned and went to run. The police, sensing he might try to get away, quickly overtook him. They were upset by having to chase after Herszle and when they brought him to the police station, they beat him with their batons and broke his front teeth.

Undeterred, Herszle escaped again, was caught, and then sent to work in the labor camp at Beaumont-en-Argonne. Although the work was exhausting and strenuous, it gave him time to think of what his next move would be.

One day, while Herszle was tilling soil, Officer Faust approached him and said, "Someone said you are a tailor."

"Yes, sir. Yes, I am a tailor."

"Come with me," Faust instructed.

Herszle wasn't sure if this was a good thing or a bad thing. He wondered if he should have lied about his previous profession. Faust instructed Herszle to march to the town square in front of him. As they neared the center of the village, Faust ushered Herszle into the home he had commandeered. Set up in a corner of the living area was a new state-of-the-art sewing machine, and next to it was a table piled high with bolts of dark-colored fabric. Herszle glanced at Faust tentatively and the German motioned for him to go over to the machine.

Herszle walked over and placed his hand gently on the pile of fabric. He recognized the feel of fine wool, and for a moment, he was overcome with the memories of sewing with Rose at their table. It seemed like a lifetime ago.

Faust's gruff voice brought him back to reality.
"You will now work here." He told Herszle that he would no longer be working in the fields but would be sewing suits and coats for his family and acquaintances in Germany.

Herszle spent his days sewing and, in the evenings, he returned to a small apartment on the outskirts of the village. Faust was pleased with his work as Herszle was producing garments of extraordinary quality. The German officer took all the credit for finding such a fine tailor. It was then that Herszle realized Faust was easy to manipulate as long as he fed the officer's ego with compliments. Herszle was repulsed by everything about the German but figured if he played the game, it could benefit him as he formulated a plan to get Charlotte out of Paris. Faust was happy with his work. Herszle was settling into a daily routine. Perhaps Charlotte could come to Beaumont-en-Argonne?

Léa and André Quatreville ran the post office from inside their home across from Faust's command post. In addition to handling all the mail and packages, Léa also ran the telegraph machine and the manual telephone switchboard. All the communications that came into the tiny village went through her hands.

Faust had Herszle send packages of clothing for him, so Léa was familiar with the tailor who worked for the "big German." In his desperation to get his daughter close to him again, he took a big chance and reached out to Léa, the only friend he had made in the village who wasn't Jewish.

After he walked into the post office one day, Herszle mustered the courage to say out loud to Madame Quatreville what he had only been daydreaming about. In past conversations with her, he had shared some information about his wife and children. He'd told her about the last time he'd seen Charlotte at the orphanage. Herszle saw the pain in her face. She was the mother of a girl and a boy herself.

Herszle took a deep breath before he told Léa he had an enormous favor to ask. "Could my daughter stay with you? I can't keep her where I live, but I will be able to see her from time to time if she's here."

Léa was taken aback by the request. After the initial surprise, she told Herszle she would discuss it with her husband.

By the end of that day, Léa had an answer for Herszle. Yes, they would let Charlotte stay with them.

"My father then had to ask the big German if he could bring me there and put me with Madame Quatreville so he could see me when he was off work."

Asking Faust was even more difficult than the Quatrevilles. Herszle was surprised when the German officer agreed to the arrangement. Herszle couldn't help but wonder if Faust said yes only because he thought there would be no way Herszle could arrange for the girl to travel the roughly 160 miles from Paris to Beaumont-en-Argonne.

Since Herszle couldn't leave the village, he asked André Quatreville if there would be any way he'd be willing to go to Paris and pick up Charlotte. André agreed; the only challenge left was how to get Charlotte safely to the nearest train station from Madame Elazare's apartment, Gare de l'Est.

Throughout his hiding, Herszle made some friends with various skills and connections, so he called in a favor to an acquaintance. That person drove a noodle truck and made deliveries throughout the city of Paris. He asked the driver if he would pick up Charlotte and take her to the train station. The driver agreed, and one morning, Charlotte found herself being lifted into the back of the noodle truck by Madame Elazare.

She settled in amid that day's deliveries and waved to Betty as the driver closed and latched the metal door of the delivery truck. Sitting in the dark in the back of the noodle truck, Charlotte thought about the last 12 hours. She'd been excited when she received the telegram the night before with the plan and instructions on how to get to the Ardennes. Still, she was nervous about the journey ahead of her, all of it in the hands of strangers.

"Monsieur Quatreville was going to wear a handkerchief in his pocket so I would recognize who I was supposed to meet when I got to the station."

André Quatreville didn't know what Charlotte looked like, and when he saw the little girl with a man who was wearing a delivery uniform, he wasn't sure if it was her. The driver knew that André would be wearing a special handkerchief in his coat pocket. When the driver saw a man who matched the description of the handkerchief, he and Charlotte approached him with caution and whispered, "Monsieur Quatreville?" André nodded. The driver gently pushed the girl forward, "This is Charlotte."

After brief introductions, the driver left Charlotte in André's care. The two boarded the train together and made the three-hour train ride to the Ardennes.

"I didn't talk. I was about 11 and a half. There were Germans on the train. I didn't know where I was going or what was happening. When I arrived, my father was not at the station because he was working."

André brought Charlotte to the Quatreville home. She was worried and nervous because she had not seen her father yet.

Léa asked the girl if she was hungry and made her a plate of fruit and cheese. When there was a knock at the door, Charlotte wondered if she should run and hide. She heard her father's voice as André let him in.

"Papa!" Charlotte rushed into her father's arms. He picked her tiny frame up and held her tight.

Charlotte felt a rush of relief. She told her father all about riding in the noodle truck and on the train. The Quatrevilles left the two alone to catch up. Herszle forgot how good it felt to smile and laugh. It had been so long that he was afraid he had forgotten how. They visited for a while longer and then Herszle told his daughter that he had to get back to his apartment.

Before he left, he locked eyes with his daughter and told Charlotte, "The only way you can stay here is to be nice and do whatever the family wants you to do. I will come from time to time to see you."

Charlotte agreed. She understood that this was the only way she could be near him.

The Quatreville home was fairly large, but they didn't have a spare bedroom for Charlotte, so they put a cot in the corner of their dining room, and she stored her simple belongings under it. In addition to Léa and André, their 18-year-old daughter, Ginette, their 4-year-old son, Alain, and Léa's mother, Marie Tisseron, lived in the home.

The family was quick to embrace Charlotte's presence in their home. Alain took to calling her "Lotte" because he could not pronounce Charlotte. This comforted her because it was similar to the nickname that her mother used, "Lolotte."

Herszle came to visit Charlotte at the Quatreville home two or three times a week. They would enjoy dinner and spend the evening together. It was Léa who noticed Faust standing in the window of a home across the street, watching when Herszle would come and go. Faust kept an eye on Herszle; he didn't want anyone in the village to think he was soft. Sometimes he purposely made Herszle work late so he couldn't see his daughter. Every so often, the girl would go and visit her father in his one-room apartment. He'd fix them a humble dinner, sing the Yiddish songs she loved so much, and then he'd wash Charlotte's hair because she still could not do it by herself.

Charlotte fell into a routine in the village for the next few months. She attended school and made friends with some of the kids of a similar age, playing games with them and picking cherries. To those children, Charlotte was like a celebrity. Most people in Beaumont-en-Argonne had never set foot outside the village.

"When I would talk about the metro in Paris, the subway, they would ask, 'What is a metro?' They had never left the village or taken a train. They would ask me a lot of questions because I was from Paris: asking me about the Eiffel Tower, what it looked like, and had I ever gone up there?"

One evening, when Madame Quatreville was operating the switchboard at the post office, she patched through a call from across the border. It was a commander with a thick German accent who wanted to talk with Faust. Most of the people in the village only knew French, but Léa also knew German. When she patched the call through, she remained on the line. As she listened to the conversation, she pieced together the orders coming from Germany. The caller on the other side was instructing Faust to round up all the Jews in the village that night and have them ready for pickup on the morning of January 4, 1944.

When the call ended, Léa, her heart racing, went to Herszle's apartment. "You have to leave!" she demanded. "Now!" She explained what she heard and told him he must also let the other Jews in the village know. She felt his only chance at escape would be through the woods and gave him the address of someone in the Jewish underground, in the resistance movement, who he could connect with. "Instead of them coming to kill you, you go kill them," she said. "You have no choice."

She also told him that he had to take Charlotte. Faust knew she had been living at their home and her life would be in danger if she stayed. Léa came up with a plan about what to do if the Germans realized that Jews were leaving the village. It would be too dangerous to travel with Charlotte. Léa knew there was a secluded farm at the edge of the woods. It was owned by a family named Fornier. Herszle could leave Charlotte there, as the woman of the house agreed to take her in.

After Herszle alerted the Jews in the village, there was a flurry of activity. As Léa suspected, the Germans realized what was going on. The streets soon filled with armed soldiers trying to round up as many Jews as they could.

As men and women took to the dense woods to escape, the SS soldiers realized they couldn't catch everyone, so they released trained German Shepherds to chase down and attack the people.

Léa had briefed Charlotte about what was happening, so she was ready when Herszle arrived. They were able to sneak out the back door, make their way across the Quatreville's farm, and enter the forest. When they got to the tree line, Charlotte's father picked her up and ran through the woods with the girl in his arms. Charlotte heard men yelling, and the vicious dogs barking and snarling, and realized the German soldiers were not far behind.

"He was trying to run with me, but he couldn't any longer. I wasn't that big but when you are running carrying a child it's hard, so he put me at the edge of the woods in a little hole near the home, and he knocked on the door, and told the woman to pick me up."

In a moment's time, her father was gone again.

Charlotte huddled in the hole, trying to make herself as small as possible. It seemed like she was there for an eternity before she heard a woman's voice whispering her name. "Charlotte, Charlotte, it's safe to come out." It was Madame Fornier. She had ventured out to the edge of her property and helped Charlotte from her hiding place.

The two walked in silence in the dark. The woman put the girl in front of her to hide her from the light as she opened the door. When she'd gotten the girl inside her home, the enormity of what she had agreed to struck her. "I'm taking you back to the Quatrevilles," she told Charlotte. "I cannot keep you." Then the woman walked out the door.

Charlotte was reeling. "What now?" she thought. She was tired and scared and wanted nothing more than to be with her father. Then Madame Fornier returned. She had retrieved a wheelbarrow from the side of the house and was placing a blanket inside.

"Get in."

The woman covered the frightened child up with another blanket and threw some vegetables on top in case she was stopped, so she wouldn't look too suspicious. She knew of a less-traveled path through the woods that would bring them to the back of the Quatreville home, hopefully without running into anyone along the way.

Charlotte lay perfectly still in the pitch darkness under the blankets and vegetables in the wheelbarrow. Her tailbone felt its cold metal bottom as Madame Fornier hurried along the rutted path. A few times, Charlotte heard voices or barking, but Madame Fornier did not encounter another person. When they arrived at the Quatreville's, the woman told her to stay covered until she came back out.

Charlotte heard muffled talking, and she flinched for a moment when the blanket was lifted from her and light from the streetlamp filtered in. She saw Madame Quatreville's familiar face and felt as if she could finally exhale for the first time in hours. Léa ushered her inside, away from the door and window.

Charlotte didn't know what to say and didn't know what any of the adults in the room were thinking. From the looks of concern on their faces, she knew it couldn't be good. All she knew for sure was that her father was gone again and that both of their lives were in danger.

CHAPTER SIX

The Cellar

Léa looked at her husband. It was as if they were reading each other's minds. Although the risk would be enormous, the couple knew they had to do what they could to keep Charlotte safe, which meant hiding her. But how? They had to make a fast decision because the Germans knew she'd been living there. It was only a matter of time before they'd come looking for the girl.

Due to the German offensive at the beginning of the war, Beaumont-en-Argonne suffered extensive damage. Although the Quatreville's home and surrounding farmland had been spared, a neighbor had not been so fortunate. That home had been completely razed during a bombardment. All that remained intact was its underground cellar.

André had an idea. He told Léa he would be back shortly and went to the homes of some nearby friends he felt he could trust. Even though it was late, most of the town was not sleeping yet due to the earlier commotion.

So, André went to tell his friends he needed their help at the farm. Without hesitation, they put on their boots and followed him. When they reached the Quatreville home, André explained his plan to the gentlemen: "We must dig a short tunnel from the wall of our cellar to the one next door."

The men set to work with shovels and pickaxes. Before long, they'd broken through the earthen barrier and made the opening large enough for André to crouch and go through. It was small enough that the Quatrevilles could push a bookcase in front of it so no one would suspect the tunnel's entryway was there.

Then André went upstairs to get Charlotte. He explained that she could no longer live upstairs with the rest of the family. "Things are completely different now. This is the only place we can think that you'll be safe," he told her.

André and Léa worked to make Charlotte's hiding space as comfortable as possible. They put down a small mattress, added some blankets, a small wooden stool, a kerosene lamp, a porcelain basin for Charlotte to use for sponge baths, and an old bucket for her to use as a toilet.

"This is the best we can do at this time," Léa told Charlotte.

Charlotte only nodded. She felt defeated and exhausted.

The only way to enter the Quatreville's cellar was through a heavy trap door made of wood located in the center of the kitchen. Léa and André placed a worn, handwoven rug over the spot on the floor to hide the outline of the door and moved the dining room table over it to further camouflage its location. They felt that they had done the best they could to create a safe hiding place for Charlotte.

Only time would tell.

The next day, tension in the village was palpable. The German soldiers didn't know who'd tipped off the Jews, but what they did know was that they had captured no bodies to transport to the camps. Some of the soldiers took out their rage and frustration by beating a few of the innocent villagers. Léa and André were worried that they would kill everyone to make an example of them all, to show people what would happen if they tried to outsmart the Germans.

No one in the village knew where Charlotte had gone.

Fortunately, the officers were ordered back to Germany, leaving only Faust and a handful of soldiers behind. Later that day, Faust paid a visit to Lea. "Look, I know the daughter was living here; where is she?" he asked.

Léa knew what he was thinking: he probably figured that if

he was able to get his hands on Charlotte, he could use her as a bargaining chip to bring Herszle and the rest of the Jews back.

Léa invited him in, "You can go through the whole home, but you're not going to find the girl."

He searched the entire home but came up empty handed.

Meanwhile just below the ground Faust had been walking on, Charlotte was in the cellar not knowing if it was day or night. There were no windows in the cellar. When the kerosene lamp was not lit, it was pitch black.

When Charlotte heard the bookcase being pushed aside, she realized it must be morning. Ginette, the Quatreville's teenage daughter, entered with breakfast. Ginette brought Charlotte fresh water for the wash basin, and she also took away and emptied the bucket of waste. This routine began a pattern. When Ginette brought meals, it was the only way that Charlotte had any idea of time.

Charlotte, only 11 years old, made the best of her new situation by playing house and creating a fantasy world for herself to cope with the long, solitary, empty hours. She invented stories about her future.

"I had a husband and I had two kids, a boy and a girl. I had a nice home, and I would take the kids to school and to the doctor and my husband had a little red car."

These daydreams gave her hope that she would survive the ordeal.

Before Charlotte had to go into hiding, she'd been a sickly child—often suffering from high fevers and gastroenteritis. Her mother was constantly taking her to the clinic or hospital. Charlotte remembered constantly taking medicine or enduring home remedies like drinking milk with a raw egg in it or being covered in cataplasm, a paste or cream made from plant material covered in a cloth to relieve inflammation. One time her mother took her to a clinic for a procedure known as 'cupping.' They placed glass cups on her skin that had first been heated over an open flame. Cupping was supposed to aid blood circulation. It seemed strange that now living in a cold, damp cellar, getting no fresh air or exercise, Charlotte was never physically ill. It was her mental health that proved to be a challenge.

The grandmother in the Quatreville family, Madame Tisseron, came down every day to keep Charlotte company. She liked to sit on the wooden stool in the cellar, so when she came down, Charlotte moved to sit on the mattress. The grandmother taught Charlotte to knit in the round, using four needles at a time.

"She taught me to knit stockings for the family. I would have gone out of my mind to stay by myself if she hadn't taught me to knit."

Charlotte enjoyed knitting with the grandmother. It helped the time go by a little better. Some days she would stay with the girl for an hour; on other days she would stay the whole afternoon. Sometimes she would bring down 4-year-old Alain, but after a bit of time playing with toys on the floor, he would get restless, and his grandmother would have to take him back upstairs.

Léa would sometimes come down to the cellar, but mostly she would stay upstairs running the post office. She did not want to arouse suspicion, nor did she want to risk anyone looking for her if she wasn't at her post.

Ginette was the one in charge of bringing Charlotte her meals which is why she knew of the girl's sweet tooth. She often asked Charlotte if there was something she could make the girl for dessert.

Unlike her stay with the Romanian woman, the Quatrevilles shared with Charlotte whatever the family was having for dinner that night. Often, it was quite a spread: roast beef, salad, bread, and fruit. Because of the farm, the family ate better than many others did during the war. Madame Tisseron also tended the family's garden as well as the gardens in some of the nearby homes that had been destroyed. The Quatreville family usually always had fresh fruits and vegetables.

When Ginette came down after dinner to pick up Charlotte's dishes, she would often linger. She knew nights were long and lonely for the girl. The teenager talked with Charlotte about neighborhood gossip. Because the girl had come to know everyone in the tiny village, Charlotte could picture the people in the stories Ginette shared.

When Charlotte asked Ginette if anyone knew she was there, Ginette always replied, "No. Nobody knows."

To everyone above ground, it was as if Charlotte had vanished. No one knew what happened, and after a bit, they stopped asking.

One morning Charlotte awoke to a day that was not different from the many before. As she glanced around the windowless cellar, she felt different—extremely anxious. She thought she might lose her sanity forever if she didn't get out from underground. Then Charlotte remembered Ginette mentioning the day before that her fiancé, Robert, would be coming over for dinner that night.

When Ginette brought the afternoon meal, Charlotte felt she had nothing to lose. She begged, "Do you think I could come upstairs and join the family for dinner? Please?"

Faust had not been snooping around for a couple of weeks, so thinking it might be safe, the family agreed to let Charlotte up for the evening.

There was a joyful feeling in the air, as if it was a holiday, and Ginette was going between the kitchen and the dining area, fussing over the table settings. She hadn't seen her fiancé in some time. He was granted furlough from the army, and she wanted everything to be perfect.

When Charlotte ascended the stairs from the cellar, she felt like with each step she was leaving the darkness behind and filling her soul with light. She began to feel almost normal, remembering the days when she stayed with the Quatrevilles before she had to go into hiding.

There was a knock at the door and as Ginette opened it, Robert burst in and picked her up, twirling her around and causing the young woman to giggle with joy. The scene made Charlotte smile so hard her cheeks hurt. It had been a long time since she had felt this happy.

They all sat down at the table and the conversation and wine started flowing. They'd all forgotten what was happening outside their walls.

A loud rapping on the door interrupted the festivities and brought them all back to reality.

"Open the door, immediately!" a man's voice instructed.

Unbeknownst to the Quatrevilles, Robert had extended his furlough time without informing his commanding officer, and now the French army police were looking for him. Fearing a soldier who might have gone AWOL, they brought German soldiers as backup.

When the family heard the harsh German demand to open the door, they assumed that the officers were there because they somehow discovered that Charlotte had come out of hiding.

Robert had a gut feeling that they were there for him, but since he could not be 100 percent certain, he quickly got up from the table and motioned for Charlotte to follow him. The officers were repeatedly pounding on the door now, so André rushed to answer it. Meanwhile, Robert picked Charlotte up and made his way to the back of the house, conjuring a plan in his head as he went. He decided they would leap out a window at the far end of the home that was blocked from the illumination of the streetlights. The plants in the garden below would cushion their fall and they could run away, and hopefully, get to the woods without being detected.

Robert clutched Charlotte tight. He whispered his plan quickly as he paused at the window to prepare to jump. Just then, a dark shadow appeared around the corner of the house. "Robert!" a deep voice called out.

In one swift move, Robert released his grip on Charlotte, and she slid down to the floor just under the ledge, as he jumped through the window. Charlotte could hear a scuffle and some shouting and realized Robert had been caught.

Outside, Robert had been grabbed by the French officer and one of Faust's men, who accompanied him to the house. He ran up when he heard the ruckus. The French officer, who saw Robert in the window right before he jumped, noticed he had an object in his arms and questioned him as to what he had been holding and what he'd dropped. Robert responded that it was his rucksack. The German officer was not satisfied with his response.

Charlotte, paralyzed with fear, had not moved from the spot where Robert had dropped her underneath the window ledge. She heard voices outside and realized that the officers weren't leaving. Then she heard heavy footsteps on gravel as the men came back around to the front of the house. Charlotte looked around and decided her only option was to hide under the twin bed against the wall. As she slid under the bed, she pushed her small frame as flat as she could against the plaster.

"We are searching for whoever was with Robert," the officers said as they barged into the home.

André and Léa looked at each other and their eyes locked in panic. They knew they heard, on more than one occasion, gunshots ringing out from the church across the street where the Germans took anyone, sometimes entire families, who'd been caught hiding a Jew and killed them. The same fate might befall their family if Charlotte was discovered.

Léa wanted to scream, realizing how foolish they had been to jeopardize their children and her mother like this. What were they thinking? Then she thought of Herszle and how devastated he would be to find out that his daughter had been caught and killed. Léa looked down and realized her hands were shaking uncontrollably.

Alain had been the only one who saw Robert drop Charlotte. He also saw her slip under the bed. His grandmother was preparing to give him a bath when the officers entered the home. The toddler had no idea the gravity of the current situation and he decided to be 'helpful' when he realized that the men were looking for Charlotte.

As he raised his arm to point to the girl's hiding place, the grandmother realized what was happening. As his lips began to form the word "Lotte," his grandmother deftly shoved the bar of soap she was holding into his tiny mouth. It traumatized the youth, but it also prevented him from giving away Charlotte's hiding spot.

Now Charlotte heard heavy footsteps on the hardwood floor. They were coming closer. Then she saw a pair of black jackboots stop by the side of the bed. She was figuring that any minute she would come face-to-face with her captor. But rather than getting on all fours to physically look underneath the bed, the man had a more insidious idea.

He leaned his Mauser K98 rifle against the side of the bed. Reaching down to his side, he pulled the bayonet with its 10-inch blade from the sheath attached to his belt. In one swift motion, he lifted the rifle up and slid the bayonet onto the metal bar below the rifle's muzzle.

He began walking the length of the bed, stopping every few inches to lean over and plunge the razor-sharp weapon deep under the metal bedframe. He figured if the blade met with resistance, he would uncover who he was looking for.

"I was so scared. The bayonet was this close [Charlotte put her hand an inch from her nose] to me. I put my fist in my mouth so as not to scream. I knew if they caught me, they would take the entire family to the church across the street and kill them. I was thinking, 'We are all going to be taken, that's it. This

is the end of my life.' I was ready to scream and say, 'Alright, I'm caught.'"

Despite all the thoughts racing through her mind, Charlotte resisted that urge to scream. When the officer reached the end of the bed, and the bayonet never made contact, he was convinced that there was no one hiding underneath. He methodically removed the bayonet from the rifle's end and placed it back in its sleeve. He mumbled to the French officer that the boy must have been telling the truth and they could leave. Without a word to the family, they left.

At the time of the search, Léa, André, and Ginette were unsure of what happened to Charlotte. They held their breath as the German conducted his search and were also convinced that there was no way she could have been under the bed. The one thing they did know was that the officers had gotten who they'd originally come for—Robert.

When Charlotte was convinced that the men were gone and her worst fear had not materialized, she slowly crawled out from underneath the bed. The entire family was stunned when they saw her tiny figure appear. Charlotte stood up, but she was white as a ghost and trembling uncontrollably.

When André saw her, his first thought was that Charlotte needed medical attention, but knowing this was not an option, instead, he instructed, "Léa, fetch my bottle of cognac from the top of the cupboard."

With his own hand trembling, he poured the girl a shot and thrust the glass into her hand. "Drink this!"

She looked at the amber liquid in the glass for a second and then drank it down as she had been instructed. The liquid felt like fire as it went down her throat. Afterwards, the whole room was spinning.

As the shock of the situation began to subside, Ginette looked over at the unfinished dinner on the plate where her fiancé had been sitting not long before. She was filled with sadness and anger.

"My fiancé was taken, and you were not!" she yelled at Charlotte.

"Ginette, it's not my fault that they took your fiancé. I was ready to be taken, too."

"Yes, but you weren't!" Ginette's eyes were blazing with rage at Charlotte.

"What? Do you want to give me up? You can give me up!" said Charlotte in exasperation. With everything she had been through that night, she didn't have the strength to fight with Ginette.

Léa came forward and placed herself between the girls. "No, no, nothing like that is going to happen, Charlotte. You have to go back to that cellar. You cannot stay up here." Then she gently placed her hand on the girl's shoulder.

The words rang in Charlotte's ears, and she felt a heaviness in her chest. She knew that Madame Quatreville was right; it was the safest place for her and the family. But it already felt like she had been down there for an eternity. Her birthday had come and gone without any celebration, and she had no idea how much longer she would have to stay in hiding. For the entire nine months that Charlotte had been hidden in the cellar, this was the one and only time that she'd ever ventured above ground.

CHAPTER SEVEN

Light of Liberation

It was the middle of the summer in 1944. Rumors were spreading through the French Resistance that Germans were beginning to lose their strongholds in parts of Europe. First-hand intelligence was reporting that it was just a matter of time before the Allied Forces regained control of France from the Nazi occupation of the past four years.

Francois Pelzer was the leader of the underground Resistance group that Herszle had been part of since his most recent escape, after Léa had tipped him off to leave the village. Their base was on the Maugre Farm in the town of Carignan, about 20 kilometers from Beaumont-en-Argonne.

"I'm sending a couple of men to scout things out this evening," Francois told Herszle.

Léa had been sending Herszle updates on the situation in the village and with Charlotte. He was concerned. She'd told him about the close call when Robert came to visit, and since that night Faust had upped his visits to the home.

Now Faust was telling everyone, "If I catch the daughter, I will catch Herszle and all the men that escaped that night."

Léa was fearful that one day their luck would run out.

Francois was sending a few of the Resistance members to investigate the current situation in the village and report back.

When the men returned, they gave Herszle a report regarding how many German soldiers they had seen in the village. They verified that Faust was still in command, and in the same house.

Herszle knew what he had to do. He was in the barn doing some maintenance on a bicycle he would take when Francois approached. "I don't think you should go alone tonight," Francois said.

Herszle knew from the man's tone that he wasn't going to take no for an answer. "All right, I'll take Marcel. But I'm the only one going into the house. Agreed?"

Francois nodded.

Herszle and Marcel waited until dark. They took a less traveled road along the woods and made their way towards Beaumont-en-Argonne. Herszle knew every way in and out of the town and figured that they could sneak in undetected along the same path through the Quatreville's farm that he and Charlotte had taken so many months earlier.

The men laid the bicycles down in a patch of short bushes and crawled on their bellies most of the way across the farm. It was a clear, cool night with only a sliver of moonlight in the sky to light the field. When they got to the back of the Quatreville's home, they hugged the side wall until they reached the front of the house that faced the center of town. Herszle looked across the square; there were no lights on at the home occupied by Faust. He also could not see any soldiers on duty, thinking to himself that they had the whole town locked in for curfew and no one dared leave their home after dark. Herszle motioned to Marcel to stay put and be his lookout.

Herszle crossed the square undetected and turned the knob gently on the back door of the home. No one locked their doors here, especially the man whom everyone feared. Herszle knew the layout of the home from the time he worked there, so he knew the room where the German slept. Herszle felt his heart racing as he entered that back bedroom. Moving swiftly, before Faust could react, he placed a pillow over the man's face and pointed his FP-45 Liberator pistol at his chest.

Herszle pulled the trigger.

The German stopped struggling.

Herszle took one more action. Then he slipped out the back door and across the square. Again, undetected.

The next morning, Léa looked out the window and saw two German soldiers headed towards her home. When they barged through the door they demanded, "We need to phone the German authorities! Now!"

Their tone shook Léa as she hand-cranked the magneto to put through their call. She stepped aside and handed one of the men the receiver. She listened intently as the man was asking for instructions, explaining that Faust had been killed. Léa tried not to react, not wanting them to know she understood what they were saying. When they finished the call, they demanded Léa come with them.

As she entered the home with the soldiers, they took her by the arm and forced her into the room where Faust's blood-covered body lay motionless. Pinned by a tailor's straight pin to the top of the man's nightshirt was a slip of paper with handwriting on it. The men forced her to read the writing aloud: "Herszle Rozencwajg was here."

They asked Léa if she knew anything about this or if she knew where Herszle was, and her reply to all their questions was the same.

"No."

They followed her back to her home, then demanded that André come away with them. Léa looked on in fear as the Germans took her husband. It wasn't until close to dark that a shaken-up André walked in the door.

"They questioned me for hours, but I think they finally realized I know nothing about what Herszle did," he said.

Both André and Léa agreed they would not tell Charlotte what her father had done. But they were concerned that without Faust, the Germans would decide to kill everyone in the village. She had received communication from another operator of the atrocities that had happened in the town of Oradour-sur-Glane.

More than 600 of its residents, including women and children, were massacred by a German Waffen-SS company.

Fortunately for the Quatreville family, over the next few days, the Germans who were left in the village lacked the maniacal leadership of Faust. They became more preoccupied with how they would save themselves during the approach by Allied forces.

Charlotte heard yelling as Ginette slid the bookcase away from the entrance to the cellar.

"Charlotte, Charlotte the Americans are coming!" she said. Charlotte was confused. She couldn't process what the teenager was saying.

Ginette grabbed Charlotte's hand and led the girl across the cellar and up the stairs. They ran across the living room floor and out the front door. As they burst into the light outdoors, Charlotte was blinded. It took several minutes of rapid blinking for her eyes to adjust to the bright daylight. She took a deep breath of the crisp September air and let sunlight fill her entire being.

As her eyes adjusted to the scene, she felt as if she was dreaming. It looked like the entire village was in the town square, cheering and shouting, greeting U.S. military vehicles as they roared into town. American soldiers were throwing candies and chocolates to the people who were lining the square.

Then Charlotte heard her name. Villagers recognized her.

"Where were you?"

"How did you survive?"

"Were you scared?"

The questions came at Charlotte in rapid-fire succession.

André and Léa answered some of the questions, while Charlotte was being embraced by her friends who thought the girl had been killed. She was so excited to be free, to be out of the cellar. She grabbed Madame Quatreville and asked, "This means I can go back to my mother and father, right?"

"Yes!" But then Léa told Charlotte that she didn't know where either of them were at the moment. Léa hadn't heard from Herszle since he'd fled that night and joined the Resistance. Her mind flashed to the image of Herszle's name pinned to Faust, and she worried about how she would find him.

"She didn't know where my father was, or where my mother was, but just being alive and being able to stay with them as a human being...it was a tremendous change for me."

The Quatrevilles went to work setting up the space that Charlotte had occupied before she went into hiding. Charlotte let them bring her things up from the cellar, as she never wanted to set foot in that space again. She had spent nine months underground without any sense of time, no celebration for her birthday when she turned 12, and no acknowledgment of the holidays of her faith.

That evening, the entire village came together for a party. It seemed as if everyone wanted to spend time with Charlotte and the Quatrevilles. They asked their own questions and heard the answers for themselves.

One of Charlotte's friends pinched her arm and joked, "You have some extra meat on your bones!" Charlotte laughed and agreed with her. After nine months of being in the cellar, three meals a day (with desserts!), and no exercise, the petite girl had put on quite a few pounds. Her added weight did not dissuade the baker's son, Michel Picard. The boy had a bit of a crush on Charlotte before the war. He was excited to see her again.

"After the war, we were still rationed because we couldn't find everything. Michel told his parents to give the Quatrevilles extra bread because he liked me."

Léa reached out to the connections she'd developed in the French Resistance during the war, but she wasn't having any luck finding Herszle. She sat Charlotte down one afternoon at the kitchen table. "You know, Charlotte, if your parents don't come back you don't have to worry, you can stay with us."

Although Charlotte was thankful to have a roof over her head, that wasn't what she wanted to hear. She worked to not lose hope about being reunited with her family as she lived a new life above ground with the Quatrevilles. Her days were filled with attending school and visiting friends. Léa let her have free reign to visit friends in the village as long as she was back home in time for dinner. There were barn dances on the weekend and Charlotte went to dance with Michel.

Charlotte always helped with chores around the house, as she'd done before she went into hiding. Her work was about to expand. One day Léa asked her, "Charlotte, can you ride a bike?"

"I've just ridden a tricycle when I was younger."

Léa brought her out to one of the farm buildings and wheeled out a bicycle. "I will teach you to ride. Then you can deliver the mail for me."

Ginette was the one who usually did the deliveries, but she also did all the cooking and taking care of the home, so this would be a great help. It took a couple of tries, but Charlotte soon got the hang of it. The only problem was that she was so tiny that the only way for her to work the pedals was to stand, so that's what she did. Charlotte began delivering the mail every afternoon after school.

"I went all over. I carried the mail to two or three farms a day. They were far apart. I loved it. It was better than being in the cellar."

The Quatrevilles were Catholic, and Charlotte would accompany them to mass on Sundays. After several months Léa suggested that they would like Charlotte to be baptized into their religion.

"I would not like that because I know I am Jewish. I feel Jewish, and I hope to see my parents again."

However Léa pressed her, and Charlotte agreed to talk with the priest.

The priest came to the house one evening and asked to talk to Charlotte in private. "Do you want to be baptized?" he asked Charlotte as he looked her in the eye.

Charlotte told the man the same thing she had told Léa, but she also told him that she would like to please the family, and she agreed to go to mass and even learned how to say the rosary in French.

The priest then broke the news to Léa and André by saying, "I cannot baptize her. She's 13 years old, and she knows what she wants."

Many months had passed since the Americans liberated Beaumont-en-Argonne. Herszle decided it was time to travel back to the village to see his daughter. Telephone and telegraph transmissions had been impacted after the war, so he hadn't heard from Léa, and he prayed that the village and everyone in it had survived. The group he was with in the underground had disbanded after helping the Allied Forces secure the rest of the area. There was an abandoned truck at the farm that the resistance members hadn't used for fear of discovery during the war. Francois told Herszle he could use it now.

Charlotte was bicycling back home after her mail deliveries when she saw a truck pull up in front of the Quatreville's home. Then she saw her father step out of the vehicle. She dropped the bicycle and ran the rest of the way. "Papa!"

Herszle spun around in time to catch Charlotte in his arms. As the two embraced, Charlotte buried her face into her father's shoulder and wept tears of joy.

Léa and André heard Charlotte's scream and came outside. They embraced Herszle and invited him in to have something to eat. His time in hiding had not been as generous as Charlotte's and the man was gaunt.

As they sat at the table, Charlotte was quick to share stories of what she had been doing since the Americans liberated the tiny village. "Papa, I learned how to ride a bike. I deliver the mail. I have many friends, and I go to dances!"

Herszle wasn't as quick to share what he had been doing with the underground. He just hoped that the subject of Faust would not come up. He knew that Léa and André must have known it was him, but he just couldn't bear the thought of Charlotte knowing about the murder.

"It's been rough," said Herszle, "and I never knew if I was going to live or die. I had to do things I never thought I would, but it was the only way to survive." Herszle looked down as he finished that sentence.

Charlotte knew from her father's tone not to ask any more questions.

Then Herszle changed the topic. "I want to take Charlotte back to Paris, but I'm not sure what the situation is there. I don't know if we even have a home left. Would you mind watching her for another few months until I can get us situated?"

Charlotte's heart broke to think that she couldn't leave with her father right away, but she understood his uncertainty.

"Of course, Herszle, Charlotte is welcome here. Take as long as you need," said Léa.

Charlotte walked outside with Herszle back to the truck. He opened the door and then turned to face his daughter. He held her tiny face in his weathered hands and thought about how she had been forced to grow up in these last few years. She was no longer the naïve little girl who could not dress or feed herself. He hugged her and held her tight and tried not to let her see the tears streaming down his face at the loss of her innocence.

"You know, Charlotte. It's going to be tough. You are going to have to do everything around the house, and I'll have to get a couple of jobs," Herszle wanted his daughter to know that things were not going to be easy.

"Papa, as long as I'm with you, I don't care."

When Herszle arrived in Paris, he drove the familiar old streets as if he were seeing the city for the first time. There were signs of war, but for the most part, the city remained intact. The Eiffel Tower stood strong, as if all along it had been a sentinel guarding the city from the Germans. He smiled and remembered a story a fellow resistance fighter shared with him. Hitler had ordered that the Eiffel Tower be torn down when the Germans first occupied France, but the order was never carried out. When the French resistance fighters caught wind of the original plans, they cut the elevator cables, forcing the Nazis to climb the stairs if they wanted to fly their flag at the top of the landmark.

He pulled up in front of 166 Rue de Charonne, their former home. He looked at the giant picture window, and for a moment, he daydreamed about seeing Charlotte sitting in her chair with Rose behind her, holding Max. He climbed the stairs and entered the building. There was no smell of food wafting down. The place smelled musty and stale. He took a deep breath as he opened the door to their apartment and gasped as he looked inside. The sound he made had startled the couple who had been squatting there.

"Get out! This is my home!" he yelled.

The man and woman grabbed their bags and ran out without a fight.

Herszle looked around at the beautiful home that he and Rose had built together. Everything was gone. There were holes in the walls and scratches on the wooden floor. He found out later that when the Jews had left the building, German soldiers came in and took anything of value, or that they wanted, and many moved into some of the more expensive apartments. When the Germans were forced out, many people searched out the abandoned apartments and claimed them as their own.

Herszle found a broom and went about tidying up the space. When he heard voices in the hall, he opened the door. There stood his neighbors, Madame Roland and Madame Elazare. Immediately they embraced, and he invited the woman in, "Unfortunately, I have nowhere for you to sit and nothing to offer you." The women both looked around the empty apartment, remembering how lovely it had been when the Rozencwajg's lived there before.

"They took everything, even the curtains," Madame Roland half whispered.

The women told Herszle they would check to see if they could find some furnishings for him.

By that evening, the women had managed to obtain a few chairs, a mattress, and a bed frame. They also brought Herszle some cheeses and a loaf of fresh bread from the bakery.
As he looked around, he realized that although his home looked nothing like it had before the war, he could add things here and there and begin to rebuild his life.

Several weeks later, Herszle received a letter from Charlotte. Her message was short, but it made his heart jump into his throat. "Papa, I have had enough here. I want you to come right away and pick me up."

Herszle knew he could not make things perfect for Charlotte's return, but he had been trying to make things better. Now he realized that the most important thing was to go get Charlotte and bring her home.

Charlotte was washing the dishes when her father's knock sounded at the door. Ginette went to answer it. Charlotte heard her father's voice: "Charlotte grab your things; we are going home."

Ginette rushed to the other part of the house, the post office where her mother was working. "Mama, Charlotte is leaving!"

Léa rushed into the kitchen and saw Charlotte packing her meager belongings into a small sack. She grabbed Charlotte, hugged her tight, and the girl saw tears in the woman's eyes.

She was so happy to be going back to Paris, to her old home with her father, but it broke her heart to see how upset Madam

Quatreville was that she was leaving. The woman had deep feelings for the girl, and after everything they had been through, she truly believed that Charlotte would become a member of their family. As Léa embraced Charlotte one last time, she whispered, "Take care of yourself, Charlotte."

Charlotte replied, "Thank you. Thank you for everything."

Herszle had gotten a ride from a friend who took him a short distance outside of Paris. Then he'd hitchhiked the rest of the way to Beaumont-en-Argonne. The last stranger who'd offered him a ride was a truck driver who was making a delivery in the area. He was heading back to Paris, so the return trip worked out perfect for Herszle and Charlotte.

Sitting on the bench seat of the truck cab next to her father, Charlotte was thinking about a recent conversation she'd had with some of her schoolmates. They told her all the things that they would like her to bring back from Paris when she returned to Beaumont-en-Argonne.

Charlotte only went back once to visit them, two years after the war. Then she told her father, "That's it." She had to move on with her life.

PHOTO GALLERY

Early Life and Family

Charlotte with her parents, Rose and Herszle, 1939

Rose and Herszle Rosencwajg, Poland

Charlotte age two, 1934

Charlotte on the terrace of her home, Paris, 1936

Rose pouring her love into Charlotte on their terrace, Paris, 1936

Charlotte, Rose, and Max, approximately two months
before Rose was taken to Auschwitz, 1942

Charlotte with her best friend, Betty Elazare, 1943

Herszle in his uniform

Camp Cadet, where Charlotte went for therapy, 1945

Herszle after the war

Herszle at a wine tasting with the Tramontane Group, his fellow
Jewish friends who served under General Vinceguerra (center)

Charlotte and Max

Herszle and Regina, Charlotte's stepmother

Ginette, Alain, and Léa Quattreville

Charlotte and Max visiting the Quatrevilles, 1945

Charlotte and Max with the Fragman family in Canada, 1958

Charlotte and Alex with their red car

Charlotte and Alex visiting Max, Regina,
and Herszle after their marriage, Paris

Charlotte and Alex on their honeymoon, Catskills

Max and Herszle visiting Charlotte, Alex, Roz,
and Marc at their home, Philadelphia

Marc, Charlotte, and Roz, 1966

Roz, Charlotte, and Marc, 1967

Charlotte and Alex with his sister, Ida, Paris

Charlotte and Alex on vacation, Laguna Beach, California, 2007

CHAPTER EIGHT

The Search for Max and Rose

Although Herszle had warned Charlotte that the Germans had taken everything from their apartment, she didn't realize just how shocking it would be to return and see it so empty. Not only was it physically a shell of what had been, but it was void of the furnishings and objects that made the apartment their home. It was devoid of half the family members whose love for one another once filled the space.

The building that had once been occupied by people who they all knew by name, was now mostly filled with strangers. The friends that Charlotte used to play with on the terrace for hours and hours—all 30 of them!—not one of them made it back to their homes after the war.

Charlotte was startled out of her thoughts by a knock on the door. She glanced at her father and felt nervous. Herszle reassured her with a wave of his hand as he opened the door. There stood Madame Roland. In her arms, Charlotte recognized the stark white duvet cover that her mother had filled with their belongings what seemed like an eternity ago.

Madame Roland handed the duvet cover to Herszle. She took Charlotte in her arms and kissed the girl on each cheek. "I am so happy to see you two!" she said. At the same time, she saw the pain in both faces. Not wanting to ask imposing questions, she quickly made an excuse to leave.

After she left, Charlotte and her father looked at each other in disbelief. They were so excited to see their prized possessions that had been safely hidden with a person they trusted for the entirety of the war.

As Herszle pulled photos out from inside the duvet, a wave of sadness came over him. He caressed a metal frame holding an image of his beloved wife as if he were touching her soft skin. In the photo, he saw Rose smiling at him. Max was in her arms, and Charlotte was by her side. It was the last photo taken of the three of them. Herszle had his precious Charlotte, but his heart ached for his missing wife and son.

Herszle went back to the orphanage to look for Max when he first returned to Paris. It was then that he received the tragic news of the Jewish children who had been taken and killed. His heart sank, thinking that his son had been part of that group. The director knew otherwise. "He never returned to the orphanage after his stay in the hospital," she told Herszle. "A couple met Max at the hospital and offered to adopt him as soon as he was well enough to leave."

They discovered he was an orphan and decided to adopt him when they found out that France was paying people to adopt Jewish children. Herszle figured, though not ideal, Max was probably safe for the time being, so he concentrated on finding his wife.

Then Herszle heard rumors that some of the deported people were returning to Paris on buses and trucks. They were being processed through the city's hotels. During the war, many of Paris' finer hotels had been commandeered by the Germans. Now they were being used as makeshift processing centers, hospitals, and one was even an American embassy that catered to the thousands of survivors.

Charlotte and her father walked several miles to the first hotel. As they got closer, they saw hundreds of people crowding around its front. Covering the walls on either side of the glass entrance doors were photos: wedding photos, photos of children, photos of couples smiling at the camera. Those photos had been posted by family members searching for their missing loved ones. Alongside the images were long, handwritten lists of names—the survivors.

This became the scene at many hotels in Paris and part of the daily routine for Herszle and Charlotte. They traveled from hotel to hotel to check the lists to see if Rajzla's name was on any of them. The metro wasn't running, so Herszle rode his bike to hotels that were out of walking distance.

Each time before he would leave, he'd take Charlotte's hands in his, look her in the eye and say, "Today, today Lolotte, we are going to find her."

While Herszle went looking, Charlotte stayed in the apartment and listened to the list of survivors that were announced daily on the radio. Days turned into weeks, and the weeks into months, but the two never gave up searching.

The two had received one clue about Rose. There was a man who tracked Herszle down after they'd settled back in at their apartment. He was an acquaintance who had done some tailoring business with him before the war and said he had seen Rose in Drancy. Drancy was an internment camp located in the northeastern suburb of Paris. It was a holding place for Jews before they were deported to the various concentration camps.

This man explained that he had recognized Rose when she was standing in line with others to board a train. He didn't know where it was going, but he had a small paper bundle wrapped with twine that held some pieces of bread and cheese that someone had given him, and he figured that Rose might need it for her journey. The interaction between this man and Rose probably took less than a minute, but just hearing of someone seeing her since her capture at the orphanage gave Herszle a glimmer of hope.

A while after that meeting, Herszle went to retrieve the mail. He saw an official-looking envelope in the stack. As he unfolded the letter within, the first thing he saw was his wife's name, a reference number, and the words "Affaires Militaires."

The letter had been translated from German into French. In the letter it stated that Rajzla Wajcberg, spouse of Herszla Rozencwajg, had arrived at Auschwitz in August 1942 and died there in January 1943.

> *"We didn't know how she died. I hate to hear that she was there from August '42 to January '43; that means she must have suffered. My mother, knowing that she didn't have her kids, and seeing kids shot there and thinking that the same thing may have happened to her kids. It's unbelievable. I'll never be able to have closure because we don't know how she died and have nowhere to visit a gravesite."*

It had now been more than a year since the war had ended. Knowing Rose's fate meant that they no longer had to search for her. Devastated by the news, Herszle realized that he could now devote all his free time to locating Max, his son.

He wasn't exactly sure where to start since the orphanage and the hospital had no records of who'd adopted Max. Someone suggested that he contact the French Red Cross because they had been helpful in locating a missing loved one. Herszle went to the office that was not far from their home and explained his situation to the woman at the front desk.

She told him that she would do some research and see what she could come up with. He waited a few days and returned to the office.

"Here is what we found. I hope you find your son." The woman produced a piece of paper with five addresses handwritten on it. They marked locations across the city that she thought may have been potential adopters.

Filled with hope, Herszle returned to the apartment to share the news with Charlotte. He also had the intuitive idea to place a photo of himself, wearing his French army uniform, in the breast pocket of his suit jacket. Since Max was only a little over two years old when he was taken to the orphanage, Herszle figured that most of his memories of his father were from when he was a soldier in the French army. He figured that this now 6-year-old boy probably would not recognize his own father.

Herszle went to the first few addresses on the list, but the children were either too young or too old. At the fourth house he went to, he met a 12-year-old boy who insisted that Herszle was his father. The child was miserable with his adoptive family and pleaded Herszle to take him with him. Herszle explained that he was looking for his own son, but if he could not find him, he would come back for the boy. Herszle felt such empathy for this young man that he asked the parents if he could take him out to the theater and for some dessert. Herszle and the boy spent the afternoon together and when he brought him back to his home, he told the boy that he would try to locate his parents so that they could come for him.

At the last address, feeling defeated, Herszle knocked on the door. A man answered and Herszle explained to him the reason for his visit. The stranger told him to come in, but said, "I doubt it's your boy."

When Herszle saw the boy, the age was right, but he wasn't entirely sure this was Max. He knelt down beside the boy and said gently, "I think you are my son."

"No," said the boy. "My father was a soldier."

Herszle reached into his breast pocket and produced the photo of him in his army uniform.

"That's my father!" Max exclaimed.

The people didn't object when Herszle told them it was his son and that he was taking him home. In fact, they didn't seem to care at all. Herszle asked for the boy's things, but all they handed him was a jacket to put on over the bathing suit bottoms he was wearing.

It was wintertime, so Herszle took the jacket, wrapped up his son, and headed home. On the way, Max still wasn't completely sure that this man was his father. He told Herszle, "If I see my sister Charlotte, I will know that you are my father."

When Herszle and Max arrived at the apartment, Charlotte was surprised to see that he had brought her brother home. As soon as he saw Charlotte, the boy ran and jumped into her arms.

"Riri!" Charlotte exclaimed as she hugged her brother. She figured that next to their mother, she was the closest person to Max.

Herszle found a long shirt for the boy to wear for the time being and then heated some soup for them to eat. When Herszle and Charlotte went to sit down at the dining table, Max slipped underneath. Fearing that he was scared and hiding, Herszle told him that it was all right and to come out from underneath the table.

Max replied, "Throw me whatever you want. I will eat under the table because they are going to come and slap me."

Charlotte gasped and put her hand over her mouth as Herszle tried to calm the boy. The people who adopted him were beggars. They made Max sit under the table and threw him whatever scraps they could afford to spare.

Herszle tried to convince Max, "It's after the war, it's finished, we are liberated, we are together, we are a family now." But Max just kept repeating that he was too scared.

This behavior repeated whenever it was mealtime and no matter how much reassuring Charlotte or her father tried, Max was convinced something horrible would happen to him if he sat at the table.

Eventually, Herszle took Max to a psychiatrist to help him work through the trauma he had been through for the more than three years he had spent with his adoptive family. The treatment helped Max to finally eat at the table again. Still, Charlotte remembered, his fears never quite left.

Charlotte was doing her best to keep the home, clean, cook, and also be a surrogate mother to Max. Max wasn't too keen on having his big sister tell him what to do all the time, so often the two would squabble.

"One time he was sick, and it was his birthday, and I couldn't bake a cake. My mother used to make bubbeleh—it's a dish that you make for Passover. I remembered how my mother used to make it. I made a little bubbeleh for him and put a candle in it and he loved it."

Charlotte also had to walk Max back and forth to school. She was having a hard time because she had not attended school from 1941 to 1944, and to be able to graduate from elementary school, she had to cover all that she had missed—four years in one year's time.

Her teacher was less than supportive and told her, "You're never going to do that. You're never going to make it."

But Charlotte was determined. Her father scraped together some money to hire a tutor to help her in the evenings. There was very little work in Paris after the war, let alone for a special-order tailor, so Herszle had to find an alternate way to make a living. He had an old friend who lent him some money, and he also had connections to the black market.

When the Americans came in, they were looking for things like cognac and stockings for their wives and girlfriends, but those things were not easily attainable at the time. Herszle channeled their requests through various connections he'd made through the black market to find the items the Americans wanted. The pay was good, and it allowed the family to start rebuilding their lives.

"After the war, we couldn't make meals the way we wanted to and there was a little café at the end of the street where we lived. They had good food, but my father had to pay the black market (to eat there). Every Sunday my brother, my fa-

ther, and I would go to that café and sit behind a black curtain, and we would have steak with French fries and salad."

Herszle kept in touch with some of the men that he'd served with in the French army The group called themselves "Tramontane," and they'd reunite at least once a year. Included in this group was General Vinciguerra, the attorney with whom Herszle had become close friends.

During one of these reunions, Herszle told the General that he really wanted to go into the wholesale tailoring business.

"You know Herszle," the General said, "you should think about changing your name."The General told him that he could help him "Frenchize" his name. Antisemitism was still rampant in France and the General felt that he would have more luck in business if he changed his Jewish-sounding last name. Herszle reluctantly agreed and the General drafted up the paperwork to officially change Rozencwajg to Rosevaigue.

As Herszle's wholesale business began to grow, he wanted Charlotte to do the bookkeeping.There were two elective classes that she could choose from in high school: sewing and bookkeeping. Herszle assumed his daughter had chosen bookkeeping as he had explained to her the plan. Upon graduation Charlotte was so proud to show her father her high school diploma.

Herszle exclaimed, "Now you are going to do the bookkeeping for me!"

"What kind of bookkeeping?"

"The kind you went to school for!"

"Papa, I went to school for sewing."

Herszle grabbed his head as if to keep it from exploding, "For sewing?!" He hired another tutor who taught Charlotte bookkeeping. In a year, she got certified to help him in that area of the business.

Charlotte was forced to mature over the last two years since they returned to Paris. Herszle felt it was time for her to learn how to wash her own hair. Rose had done it when she was little and then he had done it when he could during the war. After they reunited, he told his daughter that it was time for her to do it herself.

One day, while Herszle was out, Charlotte decided to surprise him by having freshly washed hair when he returned home. She got everything lined up at the sink: the shampoo, a comb, and a freshly laundered towel. She turned on the water and let it warm up, testing it under her wrist as she had seen her father do. She lowered her head under the faucet and let the warm water run over her scalp. Charlotte didn't realize that she had accidentally knocked in the rubber stopper, so it partially blocked the drain. She was concentrating so hard on what she was doing that she didn't realize the water was flowing over the edge of the sink, across the bathroom floor, and into the hallway.

Herszle opened the apartment door, heard the water running, and then saw the large puddle forming in the hallway, enveloping the bolt of silk fabric that had been delivered earlier that day for an important client's special order.

He turned the corner to see his daughter with her head immersed in the sink happily humming.

"Charlotte!" he yelled.

Startled, she jumped and was horrified as she saw the sudsy water from the sink as it steadily poured from the basin onto the floor. Herszle turned off the faucet. He looked sternly at his daughter. "From now on, you are going to the hairdresser!"

That wasn't the only time that Herszle realized the challenge of raising Charlotte without her mother.

"Papa, I'm bleeding, and I didn't hurt myself!" Charlotte exclaimed to her father one morning.

Realizing that he had never discussed a woman's monthly cycle with his daughter, he blurted out the first thing that came to mind.

"Go upstairs to Madame Roland. She will take care of you."

"She explained everything to me. You couldn't buy things

at that time, so you tore up sheets in pieces and she taught me how to wash them. You had to boil the pieces in a bucket with soapy water. We didn't have bleach. I was 14 when this happened, and I was so lucky that I didn't get my period while I was in the cellar."

Herszle had been thinking that it was a lot to ask of Charlotte to take care of her brother, the house, and now to help him with his business. Also, he was lonely and far too young to live the rest of his life without companionship.

"Charlotte, I have to remarry," he told her one evening.

Charlotte had been missing her mother tremendously and said, "No, no you cannot do that! I remember too much of my mom."

"You know what? I'm going to let you pick the woman."

Charlotte was horrified. She didn't want to pick the woman; she didn't want any woman!

"I have been talking to the Fragman family. They have a woman that they would like me to meet. Her name is Regine Jokubowicz. She was in hiding with them in Grenoble, in the southeastern part of France, during the war. Her husband died in a camp after being deported."

Herszle's words hung in the air. He wished he hadn't said them aloud.

Marguerite Fragman had been Rose's best friend. The Fragmans did wholesale tailoring before the war and would frequently send finish work to the Rozencwajgs. The two couples became very close and often the Fragmans would come to visit with their five children, Daniel, Irene, Robert, Colette, and Claude. The apartment would fill up with laughter and joy when the two families gathered. Rose and Marguerite would be busy in the kitchen preparing a feast while the men played cards and the children played games. Over the years, the Fragmans had become like family.

Marguerite told Herszle that the family was getting ready to move to Canada very soon. They had become disillusioned with how much France had changed after the war and they wanted a fresh start. She told him that she would get in touch with her friend Regine to set up a meeting.

Herszle brought Charlotte and Max along for his initial meeting with Regine. He figured there was no point in pursuing the relationship if she didn't like the children or vice versa. She was a lovely woman and very kind. Max took to her immediately. He was tired of his sister telling him what to do, and besides this woman could cook—eating was very important to Max. Charlotte was cordial but not happy about the situation. After dating for a bit, Herszle decided to marry her.

In her mind, Charlotte knew that her father deserved to be happy, and Regine was a kind woman, but her heart ached from the loss of her mother. The thought of someone taking her place made her feel absolutely miserable inside.

CHAPTER NINE

Rebuilding a Life

Herszle had been trying to figure out what to do with his daughter. She had been unhappy since he remarried. The four of them had moved from their old home into Regine's apartment. It was larger and offered more space for Herszle to run his business. He thought it would be a good move to get away from the old memories of their apartment, but now he wasn't sure if anything would make Charlotte happy again.

He did some research and one morning he said to her, "Lolotte, I know you are unhappy. I found a special camp for you."

Charlotte agreed to go to the camp because she believed anything was better than staying at home with her stepmother.

Camp Cadet was surrounded by a thick forest in the south of France, about an hour outside of Paris. It was created for children who had lost one or both parents in the war. In addition to the usual camp activities, there were psychiatrists and psychologists on staff to help the kids cope with the trauma that they had experienced.

The doctors explained to the children that if their surviving parent remarried, it wasn't because of anything the child had done; it wasn't anyone's fault, but it was the result of the atrocities of war. Many of the parents left behind were still young enough to go on and find love again, and the children were going to grow up, get married, and have a life of their own one day.

In fact, when they became adults, many of the children who

attended Camp Cadet in France moved to Israel and ended up fighting for their new country. They built a kibbutz to preserve their heritage and live together as Jews. Charlotte was 16 years old when the State of Israel was created on May 14, 1948.

"I was always happy to go escape to that special camp for kids. I would relate with all the kids. We would talk about our stepmothers; how mean they were and that they made us do things that we didn't want to do."

It was the only place Charlotte felt that she could talk about her mother and have her tremendous grief be understood. One of the campers told her, "If I go back, I'm going to put a knife in my stepmother!" Charlotte never wanted to hurt Regine, but she also knew that her heart would never allow her to accept her as a mother figure.

Charlotte's initial stay at Camp Cadet lasted three months. After that, she returned to camp every year, for two weeks in the winter and two weeks in the summer. In the winter, the campers would go to Switzerland for skiing and in the summer, they would travel to a beach in Barcelona, Spain.

When these trips were approaching, it became hard for Charlotte to contain her excitement, "I'm so happy to get out of here!" she said as Regine prepared her bags. At the time, she didn't realize that her being so excited to leave may have hurt her stepmother's feelings.

During her first three months at camp, Herszle, Regine, and Max visited Charlotte every weekend. During those visits, Max begged his sister to come back home. "C'mon Lolotte, come home. The food is so good!"

Unlike Charlotte, Max had bonded well with his stepmother. He had little recollection of Rose, so the situation at home was good for him. Max loved to eat, and it made Regine feel so good that the boy enjoyed the food she prepared for him.

Herszle could tell that Charlotte still didn't accept the new situation. Her reply to Max's request was, "You eat with her. I'll stay here."

During one of these weekend visits, Herszle sat his daughter down for a talk. "Lolotte, please come home and be my secretary. I need your help with my new business."

Charlotte knew that she couldn't hide at camp forever and would have to face her new life sooner or later. She agreed.

During Charlotte's time away at camp, Herszle had been building a wholesale business in addition to keeping his black-market connections. He had decided that it was an imposition to ask that his clients come all the way up to Regine's apartment on the fifth floor, especially since the building did not have an elevator and they were used to his former apartment on the first floor.

He found a new apartment building at 54 Rue de Turbigo, in an area considered to be Paris's garment district. The family moved into a spacious apartment on the third floor with two bedrooms, a living room, and a dining room. The building had an elevator, and their apartment had a terrace, so Herszle had a sign made that he hung from the balcony for people to see from the street below. The sign read: Mon Rosevaigue, confection pour dames en tous genres [clothing for ladies of all kinds].

Regine worked to make their home as inviting as possible. She was a tasteful decorator and the living room had stylish contemporary furniture, a comfortable green velvet sofa with wooden legs and a patterned design, an oak sideboard, and a hand-knotted wool rug. She even hung photos of Rose and the family before the war. Even with all of the lovely furnishings and extra touches, every time Charlotte walked into that room, her eyes went to the casement windows, and she felt a pang of nostalgia for the large picture window in their former apartment.

Charlotte was thankful to Regine for taking care of things at home. They had a maid who lived on the sixth floor of the building, and she would clean and do the laundry while Regine prepared food and helped get packages ready for shipping to

Herszle's clients. Having a routine free of the household duties allowed Charlotte to concentrate on the bookkeeping work.

While Herszle was on the road selling, she kept the accounts current, took orders, purchased supplies, or took packages to the train station. When Herszle was able to hire a couple of seamstresses, Charlotte also managed them.

During the summer, business slowed down. Most of the people in France took extended vacations. Charlotte's family was fortunate, and since the company was doing fairly well, Herszle made time for them to travel together to places like Switzerland, Belgium, Spain, and Italy.

Sometimes they would stay closer to home and visit a spa located in Aix-les-Bains in eastern France, near the border between Switzerland and Italy. The town was known for its thermal waters and wellness treatments. Max was not as interested in the spa and the treatments offered, so he usually did not go on those trips—the other three received relief from aches and pains through these special treatments. Herszle had residual pain in his thigh from the bullet wound he'd received while in the army, and Charlotte still suffered from aching joints from the time spent in the Quatrevilles' damp cellar. Regine had some circulation issues.

While staying at the spa, the three spent the mornings immersed in hot mineral mud baths up to their necks. The baths offered a mix of volcanic ash and water from the hot springs. The mud bath treatment was followed by a hot shower and then a cold shower that left the skin feeling energized—like pins all over. The final step of the treatment process was to lie down for half an hour, wrapped in a warm blanket.

Charlotte, Herszle, and Regine often stayed at the spa for several weeks. They enjoyed the mud treatments every day. Afternoons were filled with light exercises and nutritious meals. The family took vacations to Aix-les-Bains three years in a row, always returning to Paris feeling restored—body and soul.

Another time while the family was staying on the French Riviera, they rented a villa so that General Vinciguerra and his wife could join them. Herszle enjoyed vacationing with other couples and the General had joined them on several occasions. He always cherished any time that he could spend with his old friend.

One evening, as the family was getting ready to go out to dinner, the General asked if they would like to accompany him to visit a friend of his who lived between Nice and Cannes. "Come with me and visit my friend Pablo Picasso," he said.

"Picasso?" asked Herszle.

The General tried to play it off as it was no big deal to drop in on the famous artist.

"Don't worry, he's a simple guy," the General assured him. "I'm staying with you, and you're my friend. Please come with me."

Herszle agreed to the trip and the entire family accompanied their houseguest to Picasso's home. At the time, he was living in Vallauris at Villa La Galloise. The house wasn't easy to find—the General drove them through narrow roads winding uphill from the center of town. When they arrived, they walked up the stone and earthen pathway through the unkempt landscape to the modest dwelling with a pale pink facade. Picasso greeted them at the door and ushered them inside.

They sat down in the Mediterranean-tiled living room, which had smooth white walls and high ceilings. On a low wooden table was a tray with cookies and lemonade. Herszle was surprised, as he thought for sure Picasso would serve him some sort of liquor or fine French wine.

As the family was seated, Regine commented on how glad she was that the General knew where he was going, as she would never be able to find the villa tucked away in the hills. Picasso admitted that was one of the things that attracted him to this home. That and the fact that Vallauris had been a center for pottery making as far back as the Roman Empire. It was here that he'd discovered a passion for his latest medium as he watched local artisans mold, fire, and glaze their clay creations.

The General noticed a terra cotta colored pot in the middle of the table. The face it portrayed was somewhat less distorted than the faces Picasso usually painted. "Is this your latest work?" the General asked, motioning towards the vase.

"Yes," Picasso said. "I want you to pick a piece to take with you." He pointed to a row of other pots, pitchers, plates, and bowls lined up along the living room wall. All had been signed by the artist.

"I'll pick one, but I'd like to give it to my friend who I'm staying with, if you don't mind," said the General.

"No. You pick one and your friend can pick one," Picasso replied.

Herszle was so relieved when Picasso gave that permission. He didn't want his dear friend to give him such a precious gift, yet he knew the General would've done so.

The family returned home that year with an extraordinary story to share with their neighbors and with a souvenir to prove it was true.

After the vacations, business picked up. Herszle noticed the long hours that Charlotte was working, and he worried about whether she would meet a special person to share life with. Many Jewish parents liked to play matchmaker, and Herszle was no exception.

"My father was a beautiful man. He wasn't paying me to work for him, but he was buying me nice clothes, giving me everything I wanted and taking me everywhere. I think he felt guilty, though, because when I was 19 years old, he gave me this beautiful ring that he had custom designed as a way to say 'thank you' for all my hard work."

Herszle had met a couple through his business. They had a single son whom they suggested Charlotte should meet. Herszle invited the man, whose name was Nathan "Miki" Firer, to dinner several times so that they could get to know him. He was 10 years older than Charlotte (she was 19 and he was 29), but he assured Herszle that he had a good leather business going and he would be able to support his daughter.

One night after Miki left, Herszle asked Charlotte, "Did you notice that every time Miki comes over, he always wears the same suit?"

"I don't think it's the same one," Charlotte replied. "Sometimes it's brown and sometimes it's blue." Charlotte wanted this relationship to work, and she wasn't going to break it off over a debate about whether Miki owned more than one suit!

After dating for a short time, Miki proposed to Charlotte, and she said yes.

Herszle wanted the best for his daughter, so he threw Charlotte a lavish wedding at the largest venue on the Champs-Élysées with more than 100 guests.

The honeymoon period didn't last long.

The couple had been married for about two months when Charlotte told her father, "I don't see Miki going to work."

Herszle wanted his daughter to have a nice life, so he bought a little clothing store for the couple outside of Paris. Every Sunday, Herszle would help Charlotte and Miki buy inventory for the store and then he would take them out for dinner or to the theater.

Charlotte and Miki lived above the store. It was Charlotte who opened the business in the morning. Miki hired a salesgirl to "help out," which meant that he no longer had to come to work.

One day, as Charlotte was at the register, a strange man came into the shop and asked if she was Mrs. Firer. She nodded cautiously, not sure what the man wanted. He handed her an envelope and told her gruffly, "Your husband owes me money!"

When Charlotte confronted Miki, he assured her that he had just been gambling a little bit and that he would handle the debt he owed. Charlotte believed him, until more strangers with more requests for money started to come into the store.

Charlotte didn't know what to do. She was afraid that she was going to lose everything that her father had worked so hard to create for the couple, so she went to him for advice. He suggested that she and Miki sell the store and move back in with him and Regine.

That's exactly what they did.

After a few weeks of Charlotte and Miki living with them, Herszle came up with another idea. He told them, "I really want to set you up in a business. I will show you how to make skirts, how to cut the fabric and put them together. Charlotte already knows how to do most of it, and we can teach you, Miki. And I will help you get an apartment."

Herszle thought that they could build up inventory quickly as the skirts were simple to sew.

"I'm not sure I want to make skirts for a living," Miki replied nonchalantly.

At that point, Charlotte realized that she didn't have a future with this man who wanted everything handed to him. She knew how hard her father worked for his money and she didn't want him spending another dime on anything that included Miki.

The next day, Miki left the apartment early. Charlotte figured he would be gone most of the day, gambling. She packed up his things in a suitcase and was waiting for him when he came home.

"Take your things and get out of here!" she yelled at him as soon as he walked in the door.

He grabbed his suitcase and was about to object, but the look on his wife's face told him this was a fight he could not win.

As Miki was leaving, Herszle was coming in with a friend. Miki told Herszle, "Your daughter told me to get out—and by the way—thanks for giving me a virgin!"

Herszle lunged towards his son-in-law, his eyes filled with rage. His friend grabbed him by the shoulders to hold him back. Miki took that opportunity to run, possibly for his life. If Herszle had been able to grab Miki, there's no telling if he would have lived to see another day.

The divorce process turned out to be difficult and time consuming for Charlotte, but a year after Miki left, Herszle set out to play matchmaker again. He knew a couple who ran a steel foundry, and their son was a dentist whom Charlotte had met on a few occasions. Herszle asked Charlotte if she liked the young dentist and she said that she did, so he arranged for the two of them to go out.

After a few dates the man told Charlotte that he would like to marry her, and she agreed.

Herszle decided to invite the family over for dinner so that they all could discuss the situation and get to know one another better. He didn't waste any time and got the discussion going as soon as the parents and the young man sat down at the table. "You know the kids would like to be together; what do you think?"

The father replied, "You know if the kids decide to marry, you'll have to pay for the wedding, their apartment, and an office for my son to set up his dental practice. What else is in her dowry?"

Herszle was just starting to see an ongoing profit from his wholesale business, but he would do anything to see his daughter happy. "Is this what you want?" he asked as he looked into Charlotte's eyes. He didn't wait for her answer and continued, "If you want this badly enough, I'll have to sell the apartment and the business so that you can marry this man."

"No way! I'm not getting married under those conditions!" was Charlotte's reply.

"I guess there is nothing left here to discuss then," said the father abruptly. He motioned for the family to get up from the table and they all left without saying another word.

The young dentist felt terrible for the demands that his father made upon the Rosevaigues, but he could not go against his father's wishes. His parents wanted him to marry a nice Jewish girl, but they figured they would be able to get what they wanted from another family; after all, their son was a dentist!

Shortly after Charlotte broke off the relationship, he ended up eloping and marrying a non-Jewish girl. Years later, they heard that the father died in an explosion at the foundry he owned when one of his workers did not show up for his shift and he tried to do the job himself.

It was for the best that things didn't work out with the dentist. Even though Charlotte was only married to Miki for four months in 1953, it took her nearly three years, until 1956, to get the divorce finalized. Miki kept trying to extort money from Herszle. Luckily, General Vinciguerra came to Charlotte's aid, and through his legal expertise, he helped rid her of the attachment to Miki.

CHAPTER TEN

A Fateful Trip to the Laurentians

I won the trifecta today!" Herszle exclaimed as he burst through the door one evening. He liked to bet on the horses and if he had time, he would stop by the track on the way home from a delivery.

Charlotte ran up to her father and hugged him, "Papa, that's fantastic!"

"Where do you want to go, Charlotte?" This amount of winnings would allow the family to travel farther than they usually would for vacation and to be gone for a longer period of time.

"Let's go to Israel!" Charlotte exclaimed.

"We can visit my sister," chimed in Regine. Her sister had recently moved to Israel along with Regine's nephew, who was a little older than Charlotte. A plan was set in motion.

While the family was staying in Israel, Regine's nephew offered to take Charlotte for a ride in his truck to see some of the country. The road was unpaved, and the boy was driving fast. Stones were flying everywhere, and occasionally, the vehicle's back tires would lose traction and fishtail in the loose gravel.

"Can you slow down?" Charlotte screamed above the noise of the engine. She knew he was driving recklessly, and she felt he was putting them both in danger.

He braked suddenly, bringing the truck to a screeching halt. "Get out and walk!" he yelled at Charlotte.

"Take me home," Charlotte demanded.

When they arrived back at the house, Regine noticed the look of displeasure on Charlotte's face. "What's wrong?" she asked the girl.

"He wasn't too nice. He told me to get out of the truck because I asked him to slow down." She turned to Regine's sister and asked, "How did you raise him?"

The woman replied, "Don't forget he was born here. He's a sabra; he's a tough kid." Sabra is the term for a Jewish person born anywhere in Israel. The term is the same one used to describe the prickly pear cactus, a comparison that implies native Israeli Jews are tough on the outside yet sweet on the inside. Charlotte shook her head, not believing there was any sweetness in this boy.

As they were getting ready to return to France, Herszle asked Charlotte if she wanted to stay in Israel. "No, Papa. It doesn't feel stable here, and I'm afraid of living somewhere where there will be another war. I want to go home."

But Paris, after the war, was feeling less and less like home to Charlotte. The antisemitism was still high. One day, when Charlotte was going down the steps of the apartment building, someone came out the door behind her and pushed their bag of trash against her, trying to make her fall.

Then there was the time she went to the butcher shop down the street to pick up some meat for Regine. While the butcher was weighing her purchase, he casually commented, "You know, Charlotte, the Germans didn't do enough to the Jews. I wish they would come back and retake them all."

Charlotte was so mortified that she couldn't reply. She took the package and rushed out of the shop.

An example of a tipping point for Charlotte was when she went to a government office to file some paperwork for her father's business. The clerk looked at the paperwork and then requested Charlotte's identification.

"You know that you are not French, correct?" the clerk stared at Charlotte, waiting for her reaction.

"What are you talking about? I was born here; I'm naturalized.

132

Why wouldn't I be French?" she asked in exasperation.

"You're not French because you were born of foreign parents," the clerk replied matter-of-factly.

"You cannot do this to me!" Charlotte was furious. "Then you tell me what I am."

"You are an *apatride.*"

"What's an *apatride?*"

"A man without a country."

Charlotte felt her face flush as she grabbed the paperwork and left the office. When she walked through the apartment's door, her father asked what was wrong. She recounted the experience and shook her head. "France is not for me. This is it. If, after the war, I can be treated that way, I cannot take it."

Herszle tried to comfort his daughter, but he knew she was unhappy in France. He assured her that he would do whatever he could to make her happy, "I'd rather have you happy far away than unhappy next to me," he told her.

The year after that first win, Herszle won the trifecta again. Again, he asked his daughter where she would like to go. This time, she told him that she wanted to visit the United States. Regine suggested New York City since she had a niece who had recently moved there. Max would not join them; he had chosen to remain in England, where he had been for several months.

Max had participated in an exchange program, and he was staying with a doctor's family on a large estate outside of London. There, Max learned English very well and also learned to play polo and hockey. When it came time to go home, the people offered him a longer stay, which he immediately accepted.

In exchange, the doctor's son had come to stay at their apartment in Paris. This boy was less than thrilled with their small accommodations; it was a far cry from the palatial estate where he had been raised. He was pleasant enough, but before his time was up, he opted to head back to England.

So, Herszle, Charlotte, and Regine went to New York and had

a fabulous time. At the end of the trip, Charlotte told her father she would like to stay there. But when Herszle went to the French Consulate General's office to inquire how his daughter might be able to stay, he was told that since she only had a tourist visa, she could not take up residence in the States at this time.

Herszle returned to the niece's apartment and broke the news to Charlotte, "I'm sorry, Lolotte, but you can't stay in New York."

Regine saw the disappointment on Charlotte's face, and it gave her an idea. "We are so close; why don't we visit the Fragmans?" she asked. After they'd left Paris, the Fragman family had settled in Montreal, Canada. "Perhaps she could stay with them for a bit?"

At that time, the Canadian government was encouraging immigrants to come and live. Since Charlotte already knew French, they all thought that was a great idea. Regine had stayed in touch with Marguerite Fragman, so she placed the call.

Marguerite agreed to have Charlotte come and stay for a few months. She understood why she was no longer happy in France, and her heart ached for all the pain the girl had been through. "If she likes it, she can stay, and if she doesn't, she can go back to Paris," she told Regine.

"They couldn't do enough for me. I was the sixth kid there, and all the kids would say, 'Why can Charlotte do this, why can Charlotte get that? It was always, Why Charlotte? Why Charlotte?' In fact, Marguerite's last words before she died were, 'How is Charlotte?'"

Despite the kids being a little jealous, the family became very attached to Charlotte and did whatever they could to make her feel welcome in Montreal.

Her first job in Canada was stuffing envelopes for an insurance company. She didn't understand much English, so that position was perfect for her because she didn't have to interact with clients.

Charlotte had only worked there a short time when her cousin in New York told her that she had a guy that she really wanted her to meet. That trip ended up being a disaster, and when Charlotte returned, the manager asked to see her in his office. He handed her an envelope and told Charlotte it was her last paycheck and that she was being fired. It hadn't dawned on her that she had not worked there long enough to take a two-week vacation!

There was a sofa factory near the Fragmans' home called Magic Chesterfield (Canadians used to refer to a multi-seated upholstered piece of furniture as a chesterfield rather than a couch or a sofa). Charlotte heard that an accounting position was open at the factory, so she decided to go in there and inquire about work.

"I want a job and I'm good at accounting," Charlotte told the boss, Charlie Mandelson, during her interview.

"Can you speak English and French?" Charlie inquired.

"Yes, I can speak both," Charlotte said. She figured it wasn't exactly a lie because she intended to learn English quickly. "Try me for a week; if you're not satisfied, I'll go."

Charlie hired Charlotte, and there were three other women in that same department who spoke both English and French. One day, the three wanted to go to lunch together and left Charlotte alone to answer the phones. They had noticed that Charlotte didn't know much English, and they assured her that no one usually called around lunchtime, but if the phone rang, they told her to answer and say, "I'll call you back."

The women had been gone for less than five minutes when the phone rang. Charlotte picked it up, and before the caller could say anything, she told them, "Call you back," and hung up the receiver. The phone rang several more times, and each time Charlotte answered, she said her memorized reply and hung up on the person.

Charlie was in the office next door, and after the fourth phone call, he came in and stood in front of Charlotte's desk. "What's with the 'Call you back' here?" he asked sternly.

Sheepishly, Charlotte replied, "Well, Charlie, I lied. I wanted this job. I'm good at accounting but I'm learning English at night."

"You know what?" he said as his demeanor softened. "You're lucky your accounting is so good; otherwise, you would be out of here."

That wasn't the only bad day at the office Charlotte had. She had two managers over her; one was Jewish, and the other was not.

One day, Charlie asked to speak with Charlotte in his office. "Charlotte, there is $200 missing from the petty cash case," he said, looking for a reaction.

"Well, I didn't take it!" Charlotte said. She was the only one who handled the petty cash, but she would never steal from her employer. Charlie informed her that her non-Jewish manager had accused her of taking the money, and he had to call the police.

"Do what you have to do," she told her boss. She wondered how she could prove that she had not committed any theft.

Luckily, when the police came, they dusted the box for fingerprints and, as expected, Charlotte's were all over the box, but so were the fingerprints of the manager who'd accused her. Charlie told Charlotte he never believed it was her and immediately fired the man.

Charlotte started working for Charlie at Magic Chesterfield on April 16, 1958, and worked there for the entire three years she lived in Montreal with the Fragmans.

One time, when Herszle came to Canada for a visit, he was surprised at how much weight Charlotte had gained. Marguerite was an excellent cook. Charlotte remembered that often there was so much food that you couldn't see the color of the dish.

There was a neighbor who was looking for a tenant, so Herszle inquired and told Charlotte that she would be renting a room upstairs from Isador Kutscher so that she could start cooking her own meals. He told her, "Otherwise, you are never going to find a husband!'"

Charlotte's stay in Canada had morphed into three years. Her initial intention was that it would be three months, so Herszle came to take her back to France. Marguerite suggested that they visit the Laurentian Resort Chalet on the Laurentian Plateau before leaving. "I know you want so much that she should get married to a Jewish boy. Go to the Laurentians."

The Laurentian Chalet Resort was located about 60 miles north of Montreal in the town of Sainte-Agathe-des-Monts, nestled in the heavily forested Laurentian Mountains. With nearby access to crystal clear lakes and fast-moving rivers, it became a year-round playground for the wealthy from both Canada and the United States.

Herszle and Charlotte arrived at the resort in the late afternoon and decided to get a bite to eat. Across the dining room of the restaurant they went to, they saw a handsome man seated with a woman who looked like the movie star Lana Turner. She had blonde hair and oversized sunglasses. Charlotte caught the man's eye. He approached their table. Charlotte's English had not improved much, and her father knew no English whatsoever, so the father and daughter weren't sure exactly what the man wanted when he spoke to them. The man realized the lack of understanding but returned several more times.

"He kept coming over to our table, and we couldn't speak with him because he was speaking English, and we were speaking French or Yiddish."

"Why does this man keep coming over to our table, Papa?"

"I want to tell you something Lolotte: If you play your cards right (he was a gambler after all), that man is going to be your husband." Herszle was foreseeing his daughter's future.

"Papa are you crazy?!" was Charlotte's response.

"You're going to get married here, and you can come back to

Paris for your honeymoon." Herszle had never met the man before that afternoon, but something compelled him to tell his daughter those things.

The man's name was Alex Adelman. He and his wife had come to Canada for a vacation from Philadelphia. The couple couldn't decide where to go, so they flipped a coin—tails Vermont and heads Canada. This trip was a final effort to try and save their marriage. Alex wanted desperately to have children, but his wife was an extremely beautiful woman, and very vain, and was convinced that carrying a child would somehow physically deform her. After four years, he just couldn't take it any longer.

"She was a beautiful woman, but she didn't want to have children; she didn't want to be 'deformed.' To each his own!"

During their stay, Alex made it a point to "run into" Charlotte several more times, and they tried to communicate by writing pictures on napkins. Alex remembered a little Yiddish from when his mother spoke it when he was a child, but not enough to carry on a conversation.

Once, inside the hotel, Charlotte ran into his wife, who asked her, "Are you looking for Alex? He's down the hall."

Charlotte still thought the whole situation was crazy, but she couldn't deny her attraction to Alex. Besides being handsome, she noticed he had a gentleness and warmth about him that made her feel special when they interacted.

Before Alex and his wife left to return to Philadelphia, Alex asked if he could take a photo with Charlotte. She agreed and then he said, "I want to communicate with you."

"I don't communicate with married men," Charlotte replied.

"Please, I have a story to tell you." Against her better judgment and with her father's words nagging at the back of her mind, she gave him her address.

One of the first pieces of correspondence Alex sent her was

a photocopy of his divorce papers.

Herszle told Charlotte he wanted her to return to Montreal instead of coming back to Paris. Before they left the Laurentians, Herszle told her, with a wink, "Keep me posted on what happens with Alex."

The two continued to correspond by mail and occasionally by phone. Charlotte enlisted the assistance of her friend Dora Barrett, who translated French to English for Alex, and vice versa when Charlotte received letters from Alex.

During their correspondence, Charlotte was surprised to find out that Alex was one of the soldiers who stormed Omaha Beach in Normandy on that June day in 1944. He was nine years older than she was, but she never put it together that he would have been part of that historic event. Prior to that conversation, the only thing she knew of his time in the U.S. Army was that because his family kept kosher, his mother often sent him packages of food. What he never told his mother was that sometimes he would exchange those packages with other soldiers for homemade treats they had received from home. Like Charlotte, he also had quite the sweet tooth.

Alex had been in the Army for four years. During the war, his family had not heard from him for a few months and had assumed the worst. Then one morning, Alex's mother, Mrs. Lena Adelman, opened the newspaper and gasped in disbelief. There was a picture of Alex staring back at her! A journalist who was covering the war sent the photo to the paper in Philadelphia to show what some "hometown" boys were up to. The caption read, "Dugout dinner is enjoyable repast for these three Pennsylvania privates, shown in the foxhole in Normandy: They are left to right …" and there was Alex's name in black and white. Lena immediately called everyone in the family to share the good news. Up until that time, she had really feared that her son was dead.

During their next phone call, Alex told Charlotte that he

wanted her to come to Philadelphia and meet his family.

"I had had other dates that didn't work out. One guy wanted me to read a letter in French and tried to get me upstairs. Another guy asked if I wanted sex before or after dinner, and I told him, "I just want dinner," and he told me to get out of the car. We were in the middle of nowhere!"

So, Charlotte's response to Alex was: "I'm not going to a strange country to see you; I barely know you. I don't know your background."

And then, because of her past experience, she felt the need to ask him: "Before we start anything, do you need a dowry?"

She was relieved when he replied, "What is that?"

Then Alex put his mother on the phone, "Please come, Charlotte. We've heard so much about you and want to meet you. You can stay at our home."

Charlotte didn't feel comfortable staying at Alex's parent's home, but she didn't have that much money to pay for a hotel, so her father gave her a little bit of money towards her trip. Some friends of hers surprised her with the rest of the money for the hotel and her plane ticket.

A few weeks before Charlotte was set to leave, she received a package in the mail that contained a plane ticket to Philadelphia and a confirmation for a hotel reservation in the city, all paid for by Alex. Charlotte returned the money to her friends and father and off she went.

From the airplane, she saw the skyscrapers of the city below. Charlotte was excited to explore this new city with Alex. As she exited the airport, she dreamed of what they might do first. She was quickly snapped back to reality when she heard Alex call her name from a car pulling up to the curb. As he hopped out to open the door for her, she saw his sister Ida sitting in the back with a dog.

"Whose dog is that?" she asked, hesitating as she entered the car.

"It's mine," Alex replied.

Charlotte stopped. "It's me or the dog," she said, her voice trembling.

Charlotte had been deathly afraid of all dogs ever since that night in the woods in the Ardennes when her father was carrying her as they were fleeing the Nazis. Whenever she saw a dog, she was transported back in time and remembered the barking and growling of the German Shepherds in the dark. It sent a chill down her spine.

"No problem," said Alex, "Ida can take him." Alex loved dogs, but the sheer terror in Charlotte's eyes made him realize that she wasn't kidding about the ultimatum. He also realized then and there how strong his feelings were for Charlotte because he never wanted to see that look of fear on her face again.

The Adelman home was in a lovely neighborhood in Philadelphia, with kosher markets and restaurants, and close to their synagogue so Lena could walk to Shabbat services on Saturday mornings. She was a Conservative Jew and kept a kosher home.

When Lena first met Charlotte, she questioned whether or not she was truly Jewish because Lena had never met a Jew who spoke French. "You know Mom, she speaks Yiddish," Alex said to convince his mother.

She replied, "She could have learned it."

Charlotte believed Lena wasn't truly convinced until, years later, when Herszle met Lena and spoke to her in Yiddish.

Alex came from a large family. He had two sisters, Ida and Toby, and a brother, Tommy, and close to 40 cousins that lived nearby. The Adelman family would get together at least once a month, and the cousins would take turns hosting the gatherings.

Alex loved to act in community theater, especially musicals, and during Charlotte's visit he made sure she saw his lead performance in "The Pajama Game" at Philadelphia's Abbey Playhouse. The second time she came to Philadelphia, she stayed with Alex's mother, at her home, and slept in a spare bedroom. Alex and Charlotte went out every night that Charlotte was in town. At the end of that trip, she agreed to return to celebrate New Year's Eve with him and usher in 1961.

When Charlotte arrived on New Year's Eve, Alex brought her into the family room to be alone.

> *"The whole family was in the kitchen, and I was in the living room, and he asked as he slipped the ring on my finger, 'Should I ask General de Gaulle if he's going to let you stay in America and not in France?' and I said, 'You don't ask General de Gaulle, you ask me!'"*

"So, will you marry me?" asked Alex.

"Yes!" Charlotte could barely contain her excitement.

The family came running out of the kitchen and everyone was shouting, "Mazel tov!" and hugging the newly engaged couple.

The next couple of weeks that Charlotte was in Philadelphia, there were many celebrations with Alex's family. His mother threw them an engagement party, where Charlotte met cousins, aunts, and uncles. Alex's aunts couldn't stop hugging her, and everyone she met welcomed her with open arms and hearts. From the start, she felt like part of this large, close-knit family, and it made her realize how much she wished her mom could be there to celebrate in her happiness.

Charlotte called the Fragmans to share the good news with them. Marguerite told her that she needed to bring Alex back home with her so that her Canadian family could throw them an engagement party. Alex agreed and asked Ida, who had become quite fond of Charlotte, if she would like to come with them. Ida agreed, she just couldn't stay for long because she worked for the government in the supply division and always had a backlog of work after the holidays.

When the three arrived in Canada, there was a flurry of activity in the Fragman household. Mr. Fragman and his sons had removed all the furniture from the living room, leaving a large area to be used as a dance floor. The table was trimmed with an arrangement of pink and white pom-pom dahlias and gladioli. The best serving ware was on the table for the 35 guests they would host for dinner. Mrs. Fragman was busy in the kitchen with preparations.

The party was a huge success and Charlotte's face hurt from smiling so much. She hadn't danced that much ever in her life, and she met more people in one night than she had in the three years she had lived in Canada!

Later that evening, Charlotte, Alex, and Ida were sitting in the kitchen talking about the whirlwind of things that had recently happened. Ida said she had an idea: "You're engaged, and if you want to get married in the States, it will take a lot of time for the paperwork to go through. Why don't you two get married here, and then you can start the paperwork right away? It will take less time because she will be your wife."

Charlotte and Alex thought it was an excellent idea. They shared the plan with Marguerite, who told them she would contact their rabbi and see when he was available to perform the service.

When she returned to work in Montreal, Charlotte wanted to give notice because she was unsure how much longer she would stay in Canada.

"Charlie, can I talk to you?" she asked as her boss walked past her desk.

"Sure," he replied.

As she explained the situation and showed Charlie her engagement ring, he picked up the radio from her desk, a gift from the Fragmans, and threw it on the floor. It broke into several pieces.

Charlotte just sat there, completely stunned by the man's actions.

"I was going out with you, and now you're engaged?"

Charlotte had no idea that her boss cared for her in that way.

They had gone on a couple of dates, but she really didn't think the relationship was going anywhere. "How was I supposed to know?"

Charlotte said that she would leave the job early if it was going to be a problem, and Charlie said no, she was the best one in accounting they had ever had, and he would have to deal with the fact she was getting married.

After she quit, Charlie sent Alex and Charlotte a couch as a wedding present.

On January 24, 1961, Charlotte and Alex found themselves standing in the wood-paneled office of Rabbi J.J. Zlotnick of Congregation Beth Moishe. They were waiting to be married. The day before, they called Herszle and received his blessing to proceed with the ceremony without him. They also went to the courthouse and got their marriage license. Charlotte was wearing a simple dress. She'd gone out earlier that morning with her friend Dora and had bought a hat. The only people in the office were the rabbi, Charlotte, Alex, Ida, and Marguerite.

The rabbi came around his large desk and told Alex before they started, he would need the wedding ring.

"We don't have a wedding ring," Alex replied.
Marguerite stepped forward and offered to lend her ring for the service.
"They have to buy the ring from you," the rabbi responded.
Alex handed Marguerite a dollar, and she gave the rabbi her gold band.

Then, the service began. Charlotte caught Ida out of the corner of her eye. Her soon-to-be sister-in-law was holding one pole of the chuppah over the couple's head, and she was crying so hard it was shaking the whole canopy structure. Ida apologized, explaining that she was emotional about the wedding, but she was also nervous that she and Alex might miss their plane. It was after 4 pm and their flight was at 6 pm.

The rabbi talked fast, and the whole thing was over in less than half an hour. Charlotte, Alex, and Ida hopped in the car with a friend of the Fragmans and headed for the airport immediately after the service. Charlotte walked with them to the gate and then watched as her husband stepped through the doorway onto the passenger boarding bridge without her.

When she could no longer see her husband, Charlotte broke down and started crying. She sat down in the nearest chair and searched her purse for a handkerchief.

"Charlotte, Charlotte, are you alright?" a voice asked. As she looked up, she saw a neighbor of the Fragmans standing in front of her. The neighbor was returning from vacation and had just disembarked from their flight.

Charlotte wiped her tears and replied, "I just got married!"

"Why are you crying if you just got married?," the person asked, now very confused.

"Because he just got on a plane and left!" Charlotte then explained what had taken place earlier that day. The neighbor offered to walk Charlotte to the car where her friend was waiting.

When she walked through the door of the Fragman home, Marguerite hugged her.

"I'm so sorry that you couldn't go with them, Charlotte." Originally, when they shared their idea about getting married so quickly, she thought that it was so Charlotte could go back to the States with Alex and Ida. She didn't realize that it would take many months for her paperwork to be processed.

Meanwhile, in Philadelphia, Ida used her position at the government to make an appointment with Pennsylvania Representative and Senator Hugh Doggett Scott, Jr. She asked the secretary if there was a way that she could put Charlotte's paperwork at the top of the pile for immediate review by Senator Scott.

Almost exactly three months from her wedding day, Charlotte got a large envelope in the mail with all the documents she needed to move to America. She called Alex right away. "Guess what? I'm coming to Philadelphia to be with you—my husband!"

CHAPTER ELEVEN

A Parisian in America

Cherry trees in full bloom greeted Charlotte as she arrived in the city of her new home. Alex had been living at his mother's home, so the two made space for Charlotte and her things in his sister Toby's room. Alex had found an apartment for them to move into, but a few repairs needed to be made, so it would be a couple of weeks before it was ready for the newlyweds.

When the repairs were done, Alex and Charlotte moved into their first apartment at 6344 North 8th Street in Philadelphia. It was a four-story red brick building on a small side street, but it was spacious, and because they were on the first floor, they had use of a little yard area.

At first, Charlotte wasn't sure what to expect about the marriage. She was nervous about living with Alex and finally being in America alone without her father close by to offer his wise advice. Yet Charlotte was so happy because she was with the man she loved. She wanted to be the best wife she could be.

Although she had little experience cooking, Charlotte wanted to surprise Alex with a special dinner, so she spent hours in the kitchen one afternoon. In the end, the results did not resemble the photo in the cookbook. When she presented the meal, she said, "I made a mistake. I shouldn't have done it this way." She was close to tears and feared Alex would be upset with her.

His response took her by surprise: "Please, take it easy. If we don't eat it today, we'll eat it tomorrow."

Now, she was sure that Alex was the complete opposite of Miki. He had a gentleness about him that she noticed the first time they met.

"When I married him, there was nothing I could do, or say, wrong. My husband was so good to me. He was an angel. I would ask him, 'Why did you pick me? I couldn't even speak English,' and he said, 'I saw something special in you.'"

As the newlyweds settled into their life together, whenever they had a moment alone, in the car on the way to a movie or after dinner, Charlotte shared with Alex, in small doses, the details about what had happened to her as a child. No one in Alex's family knew she was a Holocaust survivor, and she didn't know if that would change their opinion of her if they did.

One evening, as they were sitting on the couch, Charlotte finished talking and asked, "Did I tell you that one before? Am I repeating myself? Aren't you tired of hearing my stories?"
Alex put his arm around her and said, "No, get it out, unload, unload."

Talking with him was very therapeutic for Charlotte.

Charlotte was working on improving her English by reading the newspaper and watching television. During the week, Charlotte worked as a bookkeeper at a furniture store while Alex was a hairdresser at the Gillette Salon. Charlotte always had the latest hairstyle because Alex practiced on her when there was a style he wanted to perfect for his clients.

On December 22, 1962, Charlotte and Alex welcomed their first child, a daughter they named Roslyn "Roz" Michelle Adelman. They chose her name to honor Charlotte's mother, Rose. When Alex went to work the next day at the salon, he wrote on the mirror in front of his station, "It's a girl! 6 lbs 10 oz 19", Dec. 22, Roslyn," then added a photo of the newborn.

When Roz was about six weeks old, Charlotte went to get

the mail and noticed an envelope from the people who owned the building. Knowing they always paid their rent on time, she opened the letter wondering what the contents would be. In it was an official-looking letter telling them that they had one month to leave and that their lease was being terminated. The building's owners had a policy that the Adelmans did not know about. It forbade tenants from having a child with them in the apartment.

Charlotte was very upset. She called Alex at work to tell him what happened.

He said, "Don't worry, my love. We will find a home for our family. It's not good for a child to be raised in an apartment anyway."

Still, Charlotte was worried. She wanted to be a stay-at-home mother and felt passionate about it because she'd lost her mom when she was young. How could they live on Alex's paycheck alone? Alex assured her that they would manage.

When she called her boss at the furniture store to tell him that she would not be returning after maternity leave, he told her that she was welcome back if she ever changed her mind.

"Even with my bad English?" Charlotte asked him.

"We don't care about your English. Your numbers were great!" was his reply.

The couple found a home at 640 Charette Road in the suburbs of Philadelphia. Alex's mother lent them money for the down payment because she was excited that her new granddaughter would only be about 20 minutes away. The house wasn't very large, just 1,700 square feet, but it had an enormous backyard. Charlotte fantasized about seeing their entire family gathering there to make and share memories.

When Charlotte first met Alex, she knew he was a religious man, but she told him she didn't want to have anything to do with religion. Her mother was the one who kept the Jewish traditions going in their home during her childhood. After the war, without Rose, it was too painful for Charlotte and her father to continue.

When Charlotte first moved to Philadelphia, Lena told her, "Alex has to go to synagogue. If you don't want to go, you can stay home, but he needs to go."

Charlotte wanted to support her husband, so she went with him to synagogue. After the war, she never saw herself embracing Judaism again, but after spending time with Alex and his family, her feelings changed. After about six months of regularly attending synagogue, she told Alex she was ready to return to her religion.

From the beginning, Alex told Charlotte that keeping kosher was very important to him, so he showed Charlotte how to keep the pots, pans, dishes, and utensils that had come into contact with meat not to be used for the ones reserved for use with dairy, and vice versa. Growing up, she never ate pork or shellfish, so that was not an issue. Alex also told her that whenever they dined in a restaurant, she could eat whatever she wanted. The couple also observed Shabbat, lighting candles at sunset each week on Friday evening and going to synagogue on Saturday morning.

Their new home was in a predominantly Jewish neighborhood. Charlotte soon befriended several of her neighbors. One day, while chatting with a couple of the women who lived nearby, one of them asked what Charlotte's husband did for a living.

"Alex is a hairdresser."

Upon hearing that, one woman articulated an idea. "Why don't you open a shop in your basement? That way, we would have a hairdresser in the neighborhood and wouldn't have to drive into the city."

The others nodded in agreement and thought that was a great idea.

When Charlotte shared the idea with Alex, he agreed that it might be a good way for them to earn extra income. A friend built a wooden countertop for Alex to put his scissors and supplies on. (That piece of furniture is still used in her home today; it holds her stereo and a television.) He purchased a second-hand salon chair and since they already had a laundry room with a sink in the basement, it didn't take long for them to set up shop.

After working all day, Alex came home to his appointments in the evening. Charlotte managed the schedule, washed the clients' hair, took their payments, did the bookkeeping, and cleaned up.

One evening, as they were cleaning up the shop, Alex asked, "Charlotte, would you like to be an American?"

The question seemed to come out of the blue, but Charlotte didn't have to think about her response. "You're not kidding? I want to be an American!" In the short time that she had been in the States, Charlotte had fallen in love with everything about America.

When she said yes, Alex produced a booklet titled "A Welcome to the U.S.A. Citizenship" (1964) that he'd asked his sister Ida to pick up for him. "Well, you better get studying!" he told his wife as he handed her the booklet.

Charlotte spent months studying the laws of the United States and working on her English. Whenever they had free time, she would make Alex quiz her. On April 7, 1965, Charlotte received her Certificate of Naturalization, one of the best gifts of her life.

"When they gave me that paper and I became American, the man said to me, 'You know, Charlotte, you are more American than an American that is born here because you choose to be American'. I was crying because in France I was born there, and they wouldn't even recognize me."

After the ceremony, Alex told Charlotte she could still remain a French citizen if she wanted to hold dual citizenship.

"No!" she said. "Throw it through the window; I don't want it!"

When Charlotte called her father to share the good news, she could tell in his voice that something wasn't right. "Papa, what's wrong?"

"It's Regine; she's not doing well," Herszle replied.

Regine had been diagnosed with multiple sclerosis a few years before, and her condition was rapidly deteriorating. Max had a strong bond with Regine; she was the only mother he had ever known. He slept on the floor next to her bed when she became bedridden. Herszle didn't want to put her in a home, so he arranged for 24-hour care for her that included a nurse to administer morphine when she was in pain. In between caregiver shifts, Max helped bathe her and tried to get her to eat.

Regine died on April 25, 1966. Charlotte could not attend the funeral in France because she was almost eight months pregnant, and her doctor didn't want her to fly.

On June 14, 1966, Charlotte, Alex, and Roz welcomed Marc Robert into the Adelman family. The stories that Charlotte used to tell herself in those long hours in the dark cellar had come true. She fantasized about having a husband, daughter, and son she could care for, and now that fantasy had become a reality.

After Regine passed away, Max came to visit Charlotte. He was going to dental school at the time. Their father told him he had to have a trade or a profession; Herszle really wanted Max to be a doctor. Being more like his mother, Rose, who was a people pleaser, Max agreed to go to medical school. There was one problem, however. Whenever he entered an operating room, he would faint.

There was a friend of the family who was a dentist. He suggested that Max go to dental school instead. Herszle was fine with that decision. France had a military conscription and Herszle was concerned that Max might be called to fight in Vietnam. Having witnessed the atrocities firsthand, Herszle knew that he didn't want his son going to war, and he figured if Max were a student studying medicine, he would be safe.

But Charlotte was concerned about her brother. "Papa, why do you push Max so hard to be something he really doesn't want to do?" She knew Max wouldn't stand up for himself, so she felt she had to say something.

"It's for his own good, Charlotte."

With that response, she knew to drop the discussion. So, Max became a dentist and Herszle helped him set up a practice in Paris.

Now, with Max settling into his career and Regine gone, Herszle decided to go and spend some time getting to know his grandchildren in Philadelphia. Charlotte and Alex had visited France about a year after they were married, but Herszle had yet to come to America and see them in their new home.

When Alex picked Herszle up from the airport, he thought his father-in-law's suitcase was extraordinarily heavy. When they got home, he learned the reason.

After greeting her father with a warm embrace and introducing him to his grandchildren, Herszle told everyone to gather around him on the living room floor. He put the suitcase down and unzipped it. The top practically flew open with the strain on the zipper. The suitcase was full of wrapped presents! Herszle sat on the floor and handed each child package after package until the bag was empty.

Charlotte said, "Papa, where is your clothing? You don't have any clothing!"

"Tomorrow, we will go buy clothing!"

Herszle joked with his grandchildren that he knew English. He didn't.

He picked up his grandson, Marc, and said, "I know good English. I punch you in the nose!" That comment tickled Marc, and he couldn't wait to tell his mom that his grandfather "spoke" English.

As the family sat down to dinner that evening, Alex grabbed a glass and poured Herszle some wine. Herszle always had to have red wine with his meal, so Alex wanted to make sure his father-in-law was happy. Indeed, Herszle's heart was bursting with happiness because he couldn't remember the last time he saw his daughter so full of joy.

He was also delighted when Charlotte said that they kept a kosher home. He knew how she felt about Judaism after the war. Even though his own faith had not been as strong, it filled his soul with joy to see her and Alex embrace the customs and traditions of the faith that he and Rose shared when they started their family.

Herszle visited the couple four times in the 18 years they lived in Philadelphia.

Charlotte and Alex loved living so close to the Adelman family. In the summertime, they would host giant picnics in their big backyard with an above-ground pool. Everyone loved going to Aunt Charlotte and Uncle "Ecky's" house. Alex received the nickname Ecky when he was a child because he'd had trouble pronouncing his own name.

The couple also had many friends and enjoyed going to Atlantic City and to the beach on weekends. Alex remained active in community theater and enjoyed performing in plays. Roz was becoming a daddy's girl (like her mother), and it made Charlotte laugh when Alex picked her up and carried her under his arm like a sack of potatoes.

Charlotte also adored their pediatrician, Dr. Bloom. He made house calls for his regular patients, but Roz and Marc were special because he would even come on a Saturday or Sunday when they needed his expertise. "I have to come to you because you don't have parents here," he said to Charlotte when she worried about being too much of a bother.

The kids called him "Dr. Bloomie," and they adored him. The problem was that they liked him so much that they begged to see him even when they had the sniffles or a scratched knee. One day, he had to sit them both down and explain: "Look kids, everybody has a little pain here or a little pain there. You can't

get your mother to run to me each time you have a little pain."
It took a little time, but eventually the kids realized that their
mother was capable of providing their basic medical care.

When Max visited Philadelphia with Herszle, he loved to play
with Roz and Marc. He let them crawl and climb all over him.
He was so great with his niece and nephew that Charlotte
wanted her brother to find someone to share his life with and
have a family of his own.

In the office Herszle had purchased for him, Max became a
successful dentist with a thriving practice and a long list of patients. One woman, Josette, often came in and spent extra time
in the chair talking and flirting with him. Max hadn't had much
experience dating, and soon fell under Josette's charm. She got
him to go out with her and even attend meetings at the com-
munist party organization she was involved with.

After a whirlwind courtship, they married. Max became the
father of Josette's 2-year-old daughter, Cecile, from a previous
relationship.

Max wanted Charlotte to meet his new wife, so Herszle paid
for the four of them to fly from Paris to Philadelphia.

One of the first things Josette asked Charlotte was, "What do
you do here?" She couldn't understand why Charlotte left Paris
to live in America. She also asked her if the reason she left France
was because she could not find a husband there.

Charlotte didn't appreciate the interrogation by Josette, but she
was polite for Max's sake.

"I was engaged to a dentist, but he wanted a lot of money from
my father," Charlotte told her. "That's why I got out of Paris. If
people knew that your father had money, they wanted money."
Charlotte was hoping that Josette would get the underlying
meaning in her message.

That evening after dinner, they were all sitting around Charlotte and Alex's dining room table talking amicably and then the

conversation turned to politics and the war. Max and Josette were sitting at the end of the table together when all of a sudden, she blurted out, "What are you all talking about? The Holocaust never existed!"

"When she said that, my father said, 'Ask your husband how old his mother was when she died?' So, she asked how old she was, and my brother said she was 32 years old and had been deported, to which Josette responded, 'She died of old age.' This happened at the table of a Jewish family!"

After her comment, Herszle could not contain himself. He lost his temper and yelled at Josette, making the point that everything she was saying was wrong. Charlotte and Alex did not sit idly by either; they added their own comments to the argument. Josette stood up from the table and told Max, "Come on, we're leaving. I don't want to stay here."
Charlotte was shocked by her behavior.

"Many of my neighbors brought gifts when they knew he was visiting, but Josette said, 'Throw them away. I don't want them.'"

Max and Josette were supposed to spend two weeks. They stayed for three days before going back to Paris.

After that visit, Charlotte would get one-word answers to her questions whenever she called her brother if Josette was home. If Josette wasn't home, Max asked Charlotte about Alex, Roz, and Marc and wanted to know how everything was going in Philadelphia. The sister and brother would have a lengthy conversation when Josette was not in the picture.

On March 26, 1975, as Charlotte was celebrating her 43rd birthday, and the start of Passover, she thought it was odd that she hadn't received the usual call from her father. She brushed aside the nagging feeling in her gut as she celebrated with her family, hoping that he had just gotten busy that day and that she would hear from him soon.

The next afternoon, a Friday, the phone rang, and Charlotte's heart jumped. She thought it was her father. She was startled again at the sound of her brother's voice. "Charlotte, your father died."

Before his words could sink in, she blurted out, "He's your father, too. Our father died?"

Charlotte was in shock as she waited for Max to respond. "How did he die?"

"He was in the hospital. He was sick."

"Why didn't you let me know? I would have come!"

Despite her shock, Charlotte was angry at her brother for keeping from her the news that her father was ill.

Max went on to explain that Herszle had gone in for a hernia operation, and a blood clot went to his heart. He was 67.

Charlotte's head was spinning as she processed the information. Then Max dealt another blow. He said, "Look, the funeral is going to be Monday and if you can come, good. If you can't come, he's going to be buried then. That's it."

Charlotte said the first thing that popped into her head. "I need a rabbi."

"I don't care. Rabbi or no rabbi. We put him in a hole on Monday, and that's that," said Max.

Max had not practiced Judaism, or any religion, as an adult, so he didn't care about the traditions of the faith. Charlotte would have to be in Paris before 6 pm on Monday if she wanted to make it to her father's funeral. She didn't know what to do first, but she called Alex at work, told him what had happened, and that she had to get to Paris.

"Don't worry, my love; we will find a way to get you to Paris. I will stay behind with the children, and you go take care of the funeral."

The news hit Alex hard. He loved his father-in-law dearly. It was a coincidence that Alex's own father had passed on the same date years before.

Although Alex had not mentioned it, there was one problem. They did not have the money for Charlotte to fly overseas.

While a friend was helping Charlotte figure out how to get an emergency passport, her mother-in-law came to visit. She handed Charlotte a check to cover airfare and told her not to worry; she would help Alex with the kids while she was gone.

Charlotte said, "I will pay you back, Lena. Thank you so much." Lena told her to accept the airfare money as a gift and to forget about paying her back.

"I arrived Monday morning in Paris and told my brother, 'You do nothing. Our father was so great to us, I'm going to do whatever needs to be done.' I got 50 people to come to the funeral. I got an advertisement in the paper. I got a rabbi, and it was done the right way."

During the funeral, Max stood in the back with his wife. Charlotte stood alone in front. She was hurt that Max wouldn't put his foot down and tell Josette that she could stay in the back if she wanted but that he would go up front and be at the side of his only sister.

After the funeral, Max invited Charlotte over to their home for dinner. At the table, Charlotte brought out some paperwork for Max to sign for the government regarding their father's death.

It made Josette irate, and she demanded to know what Charlotte was making her husband sign. "Get out of our home, get out of this apartment! We don't need you; he doesn't need to sign anything," she yelled.

Charlotte tried to explain. "It's for the government. It's nothing against you. I'm not trying to take anything from you."

"Out!" she screamed.

Charlotte left her unfinished meal, grabbed the paperwork,

and walked out the door. Max followed her and signed the papers without his wife seeing.

Charlotte returned home from Paris mourning the loss of her father, but also the loss of the close relationship she once had with the brother that she helped raise. When her father found Max after the war, they felt like a family again, even with the loss of Rose. The bond the three of them once had was so strong, enforced by the trauma they shared.

While Herszle was still alive, he paid an association from Lodz, Poland, for the plot where he would be buried in the Cimetière Parisien de Bagneux. The cemetery has a large Jewish section, and many of the divisions have exclusively Jewish graves, which is why it is sometimes known as the 'Jewish cemetery.'
There were about 10 people in Paris from Lodz. They all decided that they wanted to be buried in Paris and lie in rest among their fellow villagers, so they purchased one tomb together. Each person who passed away was buried there and has their name and photo on the tomb.
Even though Max lives 15 minutes from the cemetery, he stays away from the gravesite. There's a photograph of Herszle on the tomb, and the glass gets filthy in the extreme weather, so Charlotte pays a caretaker to keep up with the maintenance.

"My father did so much for both of us. When I go to Paris, I take care of the tomb; nothing is done if I don't do it."

Whenever she goes to Paris, she visits the site and makes sure everything is perfect. She always invites Max to go with her, and the two spend time sharing memories of their father. Even though she doesn't have a relationship with his wife, nothing can stand in the way of Charlotte spending time with her precious "Riri."

CHAPTER TWELVE

Moving to the Desert

Toby, Alex's sister, and her husband, Hans Rosenthal, grew tired of the harsh Pennsylvania winters. They and their daughters, Irene and Marsha, moved to Arizona in 1974.

In 1978, Alex and Charlotte were vacationing in California and decided to stop in Phoenix for a visit with Toby and Hans. It was February—a gorgeous, sunny day with temperatures in the low 70s—when the Adelmans arrived in Phoenix. When Charlotte got out of the car, she turned her face to the sun and let the light and warmth envelop her. It was then and there that she decided she had found her family's new home.

"Alex, this is it! We are moving here!"
At first, he thought she was joking, but when he glanced at his wife, he recognized that familiar look of determination. It didn't take much convincing; Alex, too, was tired of the harsh winters in Philadelphia—shoveling the snow—and he knew that sometimes, as a result of being immobile for so long in the damp cellar when she was young, the cold made Charlotte ache. One year later, the Adelmans moved to Phoenix.

Alex's sister Ida, now working as a real estate agent, went to Phoenix ahead of the family to find a perfect home for them. She found a townhome in a quiet Phoenix neighborhood among many other Jewish families. It was within walking distance of the Jewish Community Center and their synagogue, Beth El Congregation.

"Ida was an angel. When she saw me for the first time, she adopted me like I was her sister. She couldn't do enough for me. No matter if I said I was short on money or I needed to buy something, she would lend me the money. When I went to pay her back, she would say, 'Don't even talk about it.'"

When Ida came to Arizona to search for her brother's home, she realized the people were as warm as the weather. In 1980, she decided to join her brother and sister-in-law and moved to Arizona. Ida had never married, so Toby, Hans, Charlotte, and Alex often gathered like the entire family had when they were all in Philadelphia. They liked to go out for meals, attend the theater, and play games.

Alex was in his 50s when the family moved to Phoenix. He decided that standing all day as a hairdresser was getting to be too much. He wasn't ready to retire yet, so he asked Charlotte, "What do you think about investing in a catering truck?"

"Sure, why not?" she answered. Charlotte wanted whatever would make Alex happy, so she was game to get into the catering business.

They bought a mobile catering truck and named it the "Silver Streak" because of its metal gray and white exterior. They stored the truck in a lot of an industrial area in Phoenix. The two would get up at 4 am and drive down to the lot to get the truck ready by 7 am. Charlotte made sure everything was clean and sorted so that her husband could prepare the food and fill the orders quickly. It was hard work, but they always worked well together. Even though mornings were rushed, they enjoyed the quiet time together before the rest of the city awoke.

When her work was done, she saw Alex off with a kiss and the words, "Have a good day. Love you!"

Alex then would hoist himself into the driver's seat and head to his first jobsite of the day. He'd pull into the dirt lot and sound the horn, watching as the workers who had begun their day hours earlier put down their tools and came to get something to eat.

He liked to pick an area where he could come for several days or sometimes weeks in a row to build up a clientele. Alex always loved talking to people and he quickly made friends with many of the people who purchased food from the truck. He served a variety of fast-food items, including hamburgers, hot dogs, burritos, snacks, and drinks. He would stay until anyone who wanted food came and then he would drive to the next site.

At the end of the day, Alex would return the truck to the lot, and Charlotte would pick him up. During the evening drive home, Alex would scout various construction spots, planning where to come with the truck the next day.

One day, after talking with some of his customers, he had an idea he wanted to share with his wife. He would need her help. "Charlotte, I have an idea …" he began.

Charlotte tilted her head, interested to hear more.

"I was talking to some of the workers, and they were saying how hard it is to cash their checks. What if we cashed their checks for them?"

Many of these men working at the construction sites were undocumented workers, they were in the United States illegally. They had trouble cashing paychecks because they had no U.S. identification or a bank account. Since Alex ran an all-cash business, he decided he could have the men sign over their paychecks, and for a small fee, he would cash their checks for them.

He thought Charlotte could take the checks to the bank and then meet up with Alex during the day so he could give the men their money.

Charlotte thought this was a great idea. She admired her husband for always thinking of ways to earn extra income to take care of his family. Alex's only concern was that Charlotte would often have to drive around in some pretty rough areas with thousands of dollars in cash with her. Charlotte assured her husband that she would be careful.

The plan worked well, except sometimes Charlotte had difficulty finding the jobsite. Many of them weren't clearly marked with an address. Alex gave her the best directions he knew to give, but sometimes, if the construction site was extensive, he wouldn't be able to park the truck at the same place he had the day before; he may have had to park on a nearby street.

One afternoon, as Charlotte was looking for where Alex was parked, a man motioned for her to roll down the car window. She thought maybe he'd seen her drive by a few times and decided she would ask him if he knew another way to get into the site.

What she didn't realize was that the man had been watching her coming and going on paydays and was aware of what she and Alex were doing. He knew that Charlotte probably had a lot of cash.

"Do you know…" she began as she rolled down the car window. She didn't get to finish the rest of her question. She immediately felt pain as the man punched her square in the face with his right hand, reached into the car with his left, and grabbed her purse from the front seat.

With blood gushing from her nose, and shaking with shock, Charlotte's flight response kicked in and took over. She put the car into drive and headed in what she hoped was the right direction.

Charlotte's first thought was to get out of the area in case the man returned after realizing that there was no money in her purse. She had hidden the $5,000 under the seat!

When she finally found her way to where Alex was, his face went white at the sight of his wife's nose and all the blood. "What happened?" Alex said as he helped Charlotte out of the car.

She told him the story as he helped her into the truck. Her nose had stopped bleeding. He wiped her face with a cloth, put some ice in a bag, and told her to hold it on her nose. Luckily, it wasn't broken, and Alex promised, "If I ever see that man, I will do more than punch him in the nose!"

Charlotte couldn't help but smile at her husband as she told him the best part of the story. "Guess what? I hid the money under the seat, so he got nothing!"

After that incident, Charlotte was always careful to know exactly where she was going and to look around while entering and exiting the work sites. She stayed aware of anyone walking near her car and never rolled down the window or unlocked the car door until she had arrived safely, and Alex was in her sight.

One afternoon, while approaching a jobsite, she stopped the car when she saw that an 18-wheeler delivery truck was leaving. As she motioned to the driver to go ahead, she caught a glimpse of a man walking toward her car. As he raised his hand, the sunlight reflected on something metal he was holding. Charlotte realized he had a gun.

With the semi blocking her path, she had nowhere to go; she was trapped. The man was coming closer with gun pointed directly at her.

The driver of the 18-wheeler truck saw the crime scene unfolding. He jumped out of the cab and started yelling. Startled, the man jammed the gun into his jacket and ran. The truck driver approached the car, where a visibly shaken Charlotte sat with her hands clenched tight to the steering wheel.

"Are you OK?" he asked.

"I'm fine. Thank you so much for scaring that man off. He … he had a gun." When Charlotte said it out loud, the realization of what could have happened hit her.

The hero truck driver watched all the way as she drove into the lot to make sure she got to the food truck without further incident. Then he got back into the massive truck and drove away.

Alex knew something was wrong by the look on Charlotte's

face. "What's wrong? What happened?" he asked as he pulled her into his arms.

Charlotte told the story and Alex decided then and there that they were no longer in the check-cashing business. Six months later, they sold the Silver Streak. After more than a decade in the business, their catering days were over.

Alex took a job at a jewelry store at a nearby mall and worked in sales. Charlotte decided to go back to what she knew best—bookkeeping.

First, she worked at the Dial Corporation, headquartered in Phoenix. Then, she went to work for a credit card processing company.

Charlotte was still working on her English, but she knew her numbers, and that's what helped her progress in her job. One day, a co-worker entered her cubicle and told her, "You know what's funny? You don't talk like you write. Your reports are so good, but your English is not that good. How can you not talk right, but you do your reports so well?"

Charlotte just shrugged. She wanted to keep her secrets to herself. The woman walked away, shaking her head.

"I went down to my car on a break, and I called my brother-in-law, who was terrific with reports. I would give him what I had to report, and he would give me the correct English to put in the computer in the right way. That shows you if you want to do something, you can do it; you just have to apply yourself."

When Charlotte first started at the credit card processing company, she adored her supervisor. After a few months, she was transferred to a different department to work under a very unpleasant supervisor. That department was made up of several immigrant women from Greece, India, China, and Hungary. On any given day, one of the women would end up crying due to something mean the supervisor had said or done. It happened to every one of them, except for Charlotte.

"How come you don't ever cry?" the supervisor asked.

Charlotte looked her in the eyes defiantly. "You're not going to make me cry!"

Charlotte begged her co-workers not to give in to that supervisor. "The more you cry," she told them, "The more she is going to step on you! Don't cry. Laugh instead."

On that job, Charlotte would get to work at 6 am to prepare for the day. The supervisor often walked in to start trouble. "Are we in a bad mood today?" she'd ask.

Charlotte would reply with a laugh, "No, I'm in the best mood!"

Then, one day, Charlotte overhead the supervisor taking a call and saying to the client, "Unfortunately, there's only one person in the department now who can take your call." Then she transferred the call to Charlotte.

Charlotte mumbled under her breath, "You should have said you're fortunate to have someone here who can help you!"

The final straw came when the supervisor called a meeting. The women all gathered outside of Charlotte's cubicle. "I have a special project that I need you all to work on, and when it's finished, you will all get a raise."

Everyone looked at each other, excited at the prospect.

Then she turned and said, "The only thing, Charlotte, is you're going to have to work on Yom Kippur. So, if you come and do the project right, you will get your raise."

Charlotte had always sensed this woman was a racist, an antisemite, but this behavior cemented that fact. She felt her face flush as she tried to control the anger welling up inside her. Charlotte had always taken the holiest day on the Jewish calendar as a day off. This year would be no different. The time around Yom Kippur was also the anniversary of when her mother-in-law-passed, so the holiday held an even a deeper meaning for her family.

"Not only will the project be done right, but you will not see me on Yom Kippur!"

"I took her to small claims court, and she was forced to resign. The company paid for my lawyer. When I came back to work, the whole place knew what happened, and the people I worked with said 'Oh Charlotte, you did the best thing for us!'"

Charlotte had worked at the credit card processing company for seven years, but after the supervisor got fired, the whole experience left a bad taste in her mouth, and she requested a transfer to another department.

At the new department, Charlotte was delighted to see her first supervisor—the one she had really liked. It was a surprise to learn that Charlotte was going to be the woman's boss. The two hugged, and the woman told her, "Charlotte you really did a good job. Now you're my boss!"

Charlotte had been at that new position for several years when she told Alex she wanted to take a big vacation over the coming summer. "I want to take the kids to see France," she said. It was 1983. Roz was 20, and Marc would turn 17 in June. She figured they would soon be too old to want to vacation with their parents.

"Since we are going all the way to France," Alex replied, "why don't we go to Israel, too?" He didn't know when they would have the chance again. The two kept the trip plans a secret.

Alex left work early one day and went to make all the arrangements. As they sat down to dinner that night, he brought out the airline tickets and told everyone they would be spending three weeks seeing both countries. The kids could barely contain their excitement.

While in Paris, Charlotte showed her children the apartment building where she'd spent her childhood. At this point in their lives, they didn't know her entire history. She wanted to remember as much of the happy times in France as she could to share with her children.

She walked up the same cement steps that she had walked with her mom and held her kids' hands as she showed them which apartment had been hers. Next, they rode in the elevator to the terrace. When she walked onto the rooftop, she was transported to her childhood games of hopscotch and tricycle riding. She told her kids stories about her friends and how they all called her "Lola."

When they got back in the elevator, instead of going back to the first floor, Charlotte said, "We have one more stop to make."

When the elevator stopped, they all got out and Charlotte knocked on a door in the middle of the long hallway. Madame Elazare opened the door and let out a gasp at the foursome standing in front of her.

"Charlotte!"

Madame Elazare ushered the family into her home.

"This is my family!" Charlotte said as she introduced everyone to her former neighbor. Everyone sat down while Madame Elazare made tea and brought out cookies.

The two women talked for hours. Madame Elazare shared stories about Rose and Herszle. Charlotte had to take time to translate French into English for her family. Not wanting to overstay their welcome, Charlotte told her friend that there was much of Paris left to show her family. They agreed to meet for dinner the next day with Madame Elazare's children, Harry and Muriel. Charlotte's friend Betty had since passed away.

As they walked the city, Charlotte pointed out the parks that she played in and the theater where she'd seen her favorite Shirley Temple movies. Often, she would catch Alex looking at landmarks she'd told only him about. He knew the story behind the place had a different significance than what Charlotte was sharing with their children.

168

That evening at dinner, the kids ordered soda at a restaurant, and as is customary in Europe, there was only a little ice in the glass. Both Marc and Roz looked at each other and commented on the lack of ice. Charlotte called over to the waiter, "What's with two cubes? Can you please put more ice in their drinks?"

Charlotte remembered why she'd left France when the waiter returned with the extra ice and said, "You spoil your kids." His rudeness made her think back to how she was treated after the war: being bullied and told she was not a French citizen.

The next day, they scheduled time to spend with Max. He arrived without his wife and said, "Guess what Josette is doing right now?"

Charlotte could not have cared less, but she asked her brother what his wife was doing. "She's crying because I am here with you."

Charlotte just rolled her eyes.

"My brother is so brainwashed by his wife. He asked me why I was mad at her. I said, 'Who's mad?' She didn't even want to come and see me. I'm willing to go see her. She is the one who wants to cry at home while he's with me. But she's a good cook for him and he's a good eater; he likes to eat. That's why he wanted to stay with my stepmom. He's like my mom; don't cause trouble. I'm like my father; I push and shove."

The next leg of the journey was to be spent in Israel. Charlotte had a much better time on this trip than the first time she had gone there with her father and Regine. She felt history come alive as they visited all the sites in Jerusalem, Tel Aviv, and Nazareth, traveling from one side of the small country to the other.

Alex had arranged through the travel agent to have a car take them from place to place. At one of their stops, there was a group of Israel Defense Forces (IDF) soldiers. The State of Israel requires every Israeli citizen—both men and women—over the ages of 18 to serve in the IDF. Three soldiers were headed in the direction the family was going, so Alex offered to give them a ride.

One of their last stops was the Kotel, or Western Wall, in the Old City of Jerusalem. Considered the holiest site in the world for the Jewish people, the Kotel is the last remains of the retaining wall surrounding the Temple Mount, the site of the ancient Temple of Jerusalem.

Men pray in one area and women in the other, so the family split up as they approached the site.

When Charlotte reached the wall, she reached out her hand and let it rest on the ancient limestone. She closed her eyes and began to pray. Meanwhile, Roz had taken a slip of paper out of her pocket. Many people leave their written prayers in the cracks in the wall, believing they have a better chance of being answered at this holy site.

Charlotte opened her eyes just as Roz slipped the piece of paper into a crack above her head.

Roz smiled at her mom as she caught her glance and asked, "Do you want to know what my prayer is for?"

Charlotte told her daughter she didn't have to share such a private thought, but Roz told her anyway.

"I prayed to find a husband!"

Four months after they returned from the trip, Roz went to a Jewish singles event on Christmas night, and met Seth Goldberg. They were married on Sept. 7, 1986, and went on to have two boys, Jeremy and Jacob.

Charlotte was so happy that they could make that trip of a lifetime as a family. It was an amazing experience. Her son and daughter realized there's no place like home, especially if your home is America.

"When we came back and the kids got off the plane, they kissed the ground. When I came to this country, I thought it was gold. I love this country; this is the best country."

CHAPTER 13

Sharing Her Story

Roz and Marc knew their mother was a Holocaust survivor, but she hadn't shared all the intimate details with them like she had with their father. Roz had seen an article about the Shoah Foundation and felt her mom should share her story.

In 1994, Holocaust survivors were invited to visit the set of the historical drama "Schindler's List," a movie by director Steven Spielberg. That was when he came up with the idea of establishing the Shoah Foundation to document survivor's testimonies for future generations.

Roz approached Charlotte and Alex with the idea, explaining what she understood the process to be. "So, Mom, what do you think?" she asked.

Alex was sitting next to Charlotte and took her hand. "If you want to do this, I will be right there the whole time."

Charlotte agreed.

Roz reached out to set up the interview.

On the morning of March 31, 1996, a production company arrived to interview Charlotte and set up a makeshift studio with lights and cameras in the family's living room. Charlotte sat in a chair across from the interviewer, and Alex stood just out of sight of the camera but within sight of his wife.

"My husband was with me when I was talking. I had only talked to Alex before this. He said, 'Now, you've got it. The

story is out.' Marc and Roz had not heard the whole story, but they were amazed. The only one that knew the whole story before was my husband."

Shortly after the interview, Charlotte and Alex were at a kiddush luncheon after Saturday morning services at the synagogue. A woman approached them and said, "Hi, I'm Joan Sitver and I heard you're a Holocaust survivor." The woman shook Charlotte's hand and went on to explain that her father was also a survivor, and her mother's parents came to America from Poland. "Come, meet my mom."

Joan's mom, Helen Gries, soon became friends with Charlotte. Joan explained that they got together with other survivors through the Phoenix Holocaust Association.

Charlotte and Alex joined the organization and participated in its events. They both enjoyed going to Café Europa, a monthly luncheon named after a café in Stockholm, Sweden where survivors would meet to try to locate missing family members and friends after the war.

Even though each survivor's story was unique and different from Charlotte's, she looked forward to gathering with these people who understood what she'd been through. She listened to their stories, but she was still uncomfortable about talking about her own experiences. She still only shared her most intimate thoughts and feelings with Alex.

"Is it all right that I only tell you my stories?" Charlotte asked Alex one Saturday morning as they were getting ready to leave for services at Beth El. "Some survivors talk to big groups."

"Whatever you are comfortable with, my love," was his response. "Now, let's get ready to go." Alex liked to get to the synagogue when it started at 9 in the morning.

"You know, Alex, we could get there around 10 or 10:30," suggested Charlotte. But that never worked.

"If we go to synagogue, we go when it starts," was his reply.

Charlotte's brother Max had a bar mitzvah in France after the war, but since France only acknowledged Orthodox Judaism at the time, not Reform or Conservative Judaism, girls weren't honored with the same tradition.

"Women in France were looked down on. They were supposed to be in the kitchen, not talking with men, just cooking and taking care of the kids. When I came to America, there was a very big difference. Even in Canada, the women weren't at the same level as men."

So, when Beth El Congregation Cantor Sam Goldman suggested that Charlotte have a bat mitzvah as an adult, she was delighted. Cantor Goldman had also mentored Marc to prepare for his bar mitzvah.

"There were 12 of us when we started to study, and only one man and I made it to the end. Everyone else dropped out! It took about a year and a half of studying. If you know Hebrew, it's easier; I didn't know one word of Hebrew. That made me follow through to becoming more active."

Cantor Goldman had a tip for Charlotte. "When you come up to the bimah, and you do the prayer, it looks like the second line and the first line are the same, but they're not. One is pronounced 'barchu' and the second line is pronounced 'baruch.' Everyone says baruch and baruch but it's barchu and baruch."

He explained the lines went like this:

"Ba-r'chu et a-do-nai ha-m'vo-rach. Bless the Lord who is blessed."

"Ba-ruch a-do-nai ha-m'vo-rach l'o-lahm va-ed. Blessed be the Lord who is blessed for all eternity."

"It's always in my memory when I go to synagogue, and I have an aliyah. I say the prayer and I think of him."

On June 2, 2006, a 74-year-old Charlotte nervously approached the bimah. She started to read from the Torah, "ba-r'chu et a-do-nai …" and looked towards Cantor Goldman and smiled as she remembered to recite the next line correctly, starting with "ba-ruch a-do-nai …"

Cantor Goldman nodded and smiled back.

She looked over to Alex next. He was beaming with pride as a tear escaped his eye and rolled down his cheek. As she continued reading from the Torah, Charlotte glanced up at the rest of her family: Marc, Roz, and Seth, as well as her grandsons, Jacob and Jeremy.

After the ceremony, Alex was the first one to embrace Charlotte, "I am so proud of you!" He knew how hard she had worked to get to this point, studying two to three times a week.

Cantor Goldman was also pleased with how well Charlotte recited her prayers. He had grown very fond of Charlotte.

Little did he know that in less than five years, he would be presiding over Alex's funeral because Rabbi Arthur Lavinsky would be out of town.

Alex had had surgery for colon cancer and was lucky to have spent 10 more years with his family before a stroke and complications from diabetes robbed him of his health.

When Alex was in the hospital, Charlotte brought him a kosher meal in the evening and spent the night on a reclining chair next to his hospital bed. She was there to help him during the night when the nurses didn't come quick enough. She also brought in breakfast; then she would leave to go home, shower, and nap until Roz or one of her friends picked up a kosher lunch, and they'd bring it to him.

When their Rabbi Lavinsky would come to the hospital to visit, he always commented that he knew Alex was in good hands because Charlotte was there.

Alex wanted to leave the hospital and stay at home, so Charlotte took care of him and arranged for hospice to assist her.

Every time she entered the room, he would muster a smile. She would give him a tender touch on the hand or a kiss on the forehead.

"His body let go. For two years, I had hospice come in. I didn't want to put him in a home. I didn't want them to say they were with hospice, so I said that they were with Medicare. He would say, 'Who are these people?' and I would say, 'They are with Medicare.' He knew hospice came in if you were dying but I didn't want to make him feel that he was dying. The doctor came a couple of times and told me, 'You could be my nurse the way that you take care of your husband.' Hospice took care of everything; it was the best. He died at home; it was good."

On Sunday, May 22, 2011, Alexander Adelman passed away at home, surrounded by his family. Graveside services were held on May 24, and after the service, the family accepted visitors at the clubhouse of the Adelman's home development. As was customary, the family sat shiva at Charlotte's home for the rest of the week.

It all seemed like a bad dream to Charlotte. She was preparing herself for Alex's death, but she didn't know how devastating the loss would feel. In January 2011, the couple had celebrated their 50th anniversary. She kept expecting to see him in the house when she turned a corner or hear him cracking a joke like he used to do, trying to make her laugh.

When they made up their wills, they had decided that their headstone would have their given names and nicknames on it. Alex would have "Ecky," the name he called himself when he was younger and couldn't pronounce Alex, and Charlotte would have "Lola," the name the children on the terrace called her because they couldn't pronounce "Lolotte." Her side was to say, "Loving wife, mother & Meme" for the nickname her grandchildren called her, and his side was to say, "Loving husband, father & Pop Pop," for what the grandkids called him.

Charlotte made a shadow box with the jacket from Alex's army uniform and the American flag that had been draped on his casket. When she looked at it hanging on the wall across from the kitchen, it gave her a bit of comfort, like he was still there. On the opposite wall, she had a photo of the two of them in front of the Hotel del Coronado, one of their favorite vacation spots.

She also got up every Monday, Thursday, Friday, and Saturday and went to synagogue to say the Mourner's Kaddish, a traditional Jewish prayer said for a deceased loved one. Although the prayer never mentions death, it praises God and concludes with a plea for universal peace. The prayer is said with a minyan, a group of ten adults required for certain religious obligations.

"Charlotte, you've been coming almost a year, saying Kaddish for Alex. Why don't you help us say Kaddish for other people?" Cantor Goldman asked her.

"It gives me a sense of purpose to get up and come here," said Charlotte. Otherwise, she would just lie in bed wondering how to spend her day. She agreed to come to be part of the minyan to say Kaddish for others.

Roz knew her mom going to synagogue was healing, but she thought maybe she needed some additional help to process her grief. "I think it might be good if you go to a support group for widows," she suggested. At first, Charlotte was reluctant to go to talk in front of a group of people, so a therapist came to the house every other week to talk one-on-one with her.

"The widows' support group helped me a lot. The therapist made me go to groups, and I talked a little bit about my husband and the life I had. It's sad, but I have to go on for my children; it strengthened me."

Charlotte also started telling more details of her story to her sisters-in-law. Alex had respected her wishes throughout their marriage and didn't divulge any details about what Charlotte had been through during the war. The women always listened when Charlotte wanted to talk about things. Ida didn't push her after she shared horrific stories from her childhood, and Toby was always surprised, but also respected Charlotte and let her take the lead.

Marc and Roz had learned so much through the Spielberg project about what their mother had been through, but they were always in shock when she explained more of the specific facts.

"Why didn't you tell us any of this before?" Marc asked.

"I was telling Daddy, and I felt it was fulfilling me just telling him. In fact, I was always repeating myself and I would say, 'Oh Alex, I think I told you that story many times—the same thing—and he would say, 'Unload, unload.' That was my therapy."

"You have nobody to talk to now. What about going to different places and telling your story?" Roz suggested.

"Joan had approached me in synagogue the other day and asked if I would like to do that," said Charlotte. Joan was now president of the Phoenix Holocaust Association and thought, with Alex gone, it would be good for Charlotte to share her story with others.

"That's how I started. She gave me a couple of schools to talk at, and my daughter came along. It worked out pretty good, so I felt that I could do more. As I tell it, it wears me down when I'm finished. But when I think about the impact, when I feel I can do something for somebody, that strengthens me."

One of the first schools she visited and spoke at was a charter school in Phoenix that helps kids with challenges; kids who had not had success in a traditional learning environment.

When Charlotte, Marc, and Roz's mother-in-law, Elaine, who came for support, arrived at the school, there were about 80 kids waiting in the room to hear her speak. They were loud and rambunctious.

The principal of the school spoke to her in private before he introduced her to the students. "I don't know what is going to happen," he told her, "They are not like the students you may be used to talking to." He explained that many have difficult home lives, and some are homeless.

Charlotte shrugged off his words and told him she would do her best.

When she started talking, she immediately had all the students' attention. Just like the other school groups she had spoken to; the room became silent as Charlotte shared the astounding events that comprised her childhood.

At the end of her talk, she showed photos to prove the validity of her remarkable stories. Then, she answered questions, as the students always have questions.

One girl asked, "How come you don't read off a paper when you talk?"

"It comes naturally to me because it happened to me. It's in my flesh. The Germans didn't get me, but they brand(ed) me," said Charlotte. "Sometimes I have dreams, and I'm right back there. I wake up and think, 'Oh it's just a dream.' I go to bed with it; I wake up with it. It's always there."

One girl had a comment for Charlotte: "I could never be so courageous like you. I would give up," she said as she was fighting back tears.

"When you're against the wall, you do anything you can," Charlotte replied.

A boy stood up and asked, "What's your favorite food?"

"Dessert...because I am not sweet enough!" Charlotte joked.

One boy had gone outside, where his grandfather had been waiting in the car to pick him up, and told him he should come inside, listen to Charlotte's story, and meet her. "It was an incredible story, thank you for sharing it with my grandson and the other students," the man said.

"It's my pleasure," responded Charlotte.

After the talk, some of the kids came up to give Charlotte a hug or take a selfie with her.

When the crowd had dispersed, the principal came up and told her, "You did a fabulous job! I didn't recognize my students!"

Charlotte was so happy. That talk remained one of her favorite speaking engagements, even after talking to thousands of students and adults at venues that ranged from churches to an Air Force base.

"It's unbelievable that I can touch kids like that. That makes me feel like I'm bringing something to the table. I never thought when I was in the cellar that I would go and tell my story like this."

One of the largest audiences Charlotte was asked to address was at the Scottsdale Center for the Performing Arts for a Violins of Hope Tribute Concert on March 19, 2019. Violins of Hope were instruments that helped those in concentration camps escape the darkness of the moment and replace it with hope through the language of music.

A traveling exhibit of the instruments was on display in Arizona from February through March of that year, and events included lectures, concerts, and educational programs.

The particular event Charlotte was scheduled to speak at was a concert featuring musicians playing the historic instruments interwoven with Holocaust survivors sharing their stories. The evening was emceed by a local newscaster, Lin Sue Cooney.

Since Charlotte would not have the usual hour or more to talk, she met with Lin Sue prior to the concert to review an abbreviated version and essential talking points.

The afternoon of the event, Roz called Charlotte and said, "Mom, I'm going to drive you tonight. It'll be dark when you're done, and I know you don't like driving in the dark. I want you to be safe."

"No, Roz, I'll be fine. I'll pick up Marc, and we'll go," was Charlotte's response.

Roz insisted.

The concert was set to start at 7:30 pm, but preferring to be early, Charlotte insisted Roz pick her up at 6 pm, and then they would pick up Marc.

With Roz driving, Marc in the passenger seat, and Charlotte in the back of Roz's Tesla, they started the 30-minute drive to Scottsdale. Charlotte was talking to Marc when she heard the screech of breaks and the loud sound of scraping metal as the airbag exploded into her.

Someone in an SUV had made a left-hand turn into them and hit the Tesla so hard it was forced over the curb and into a light pole. The front of the car was turned into a crumbled mass of metal.

"When the accident happened, I was thinking, 'We are finished. I'm dead.' I couldn't see anything; I couldn't hear any-thing because I lost one of my hearing aids. When they took me out, they wanted to put me in the ambulance. I said, 'No, I'm going to a show.'"

Luckily, no one appeared to be injured. Charlotte said her neck hurt, and the paramedics kept telling her, "Let's just go to the hospital and get checked out."

Charlotte told them point blank, "No, I have a show; I have a lot of people waiting for me. I made a promise to be there."

Roz knew she would not win this argument with her mother, so she called her son Jacob to come and take Marc and Charlotte to the event. Still terribly shaken up from the accident, Seth came and picked up Roz and brought her home.

Jacob told her, "Meme, as soon as you are done, I am taking you to the hospital, OK?" Jacob knew he had to use this as a bargaining tool before he agreed to take her to the show.

"OK, OK, let's go!" was Charlotte's response.

When she got to the event, she told a few people what happened and they said, "Why don't you go to the hospital? Why are you here?"

After hearing the details of the accident, Lin Sue asked, "Are you sure you're going to be able to talk?"

"I promised I was going to do this," Charlotte responded.

As she walked through the crowd to her seat, people who recognized her went to embrace her and she put up her hand. "Please, no, I was in a car accident."

She, Marc, and Jacob sat in the front row for an hour, listening to the violinists perform before it was her turn to speak. Charlotte was experiencing excruciating pain in her neck, and she thought she must have really twisted it when the airbag hit her.

When it was her turn, she walked up on stage and sat down next to Lin Sue. The emcee wanted to tell the audience what happened, but Charlotte asked her not to.

Lin Sue gave a brief account of Charlotte's biography, and then asked her questions. All the while, Lin Sue held Charlotte's hand and would give her a gentle squeeze of reassurance as she talked.

When her interview concluded, Charlotte stood up to thunderous applause from the audience. Relief that she had fulfilled her promise set in, and as the adrenaline that had been keeping her going throughout the evening subsided, she realized just how exhausted she was. Marc and Jacob were there when she got off the stage, and they all agreed it would be best if they left.

"Remember our agreement, Meme. We are going to the hospital," said Jacob as he held the car door open for his grandmother.

"Yes, yes, I remember," she said.

Jacob parked near the entrance to the emergency room and he and Marc helped Charlotte out of the car. They walked arm in arm into the hospital. As they walked up to the admitting desk, Charlotte glanced over at the waiting area. About 40 people were sitting in the chairs.

She nudged Jacob and pointed to the throng of people. "I am so tired; let's come back first thing in the morning, OK?"

Jacob looked at the crowd and down at his grandmother. He figured if she wanted to go home, there wasn't a whole lot he could do to stop her at this point, so he agreed to pick her up the following day and bring her back.

He brought her home and walked her to the door. "Are you sure you are all right, Meme?"

"I'll be fine," Charlotte assured him. "Love you, goodnight."

Charlotte went inside, took some Tylenol, and had a very restless night.

The next morning, Jacob arrived as promised. They went to the hospital near Charlotte's house. When they arrived at 8 am, she was seen immediately.

A nurse came in first and asked Charlotte what happened. She explained the accident and told her that she must have twisted her neck because it was very painful. The next person who came in was the X-ray technician who took several X-rays of Charlotte's neck.

After what seemed like forever, Charlotte finally saw the doctor.

"Well, Mrs. Adelman, you didn't twist your neck; you fractured the bone."

"I broke my neck?!" Charlotte couldn't believe what she was hearing.

"Yes, yes, you did." The doctor went on to explain that he wanted her to be admitted and stay in the hospital for a couple of days to make sure there were no complications due to her age. Charlotte was just shy of her 87th birthday and had osteoporosis.

Sitting in the hospital bed that evening, with a neck brace on, and having an intravenous line supplying painkillers, the reality that she had broken her neck really hit her. She felt like, once again, someone was watching over her from above and that it was a miracle that they all weren't killed.

When Roz came to visit a little later, she told her that the car had been totaled. "The officer said if it weren't for the Tesla, we would have been killed. The person who hit us was in a big SUV and they weren't hurt at all. Another car we all would have been killed," Roz said, tears rolling down her cheeks as she locked eyes with her mom.

After two days in the hospital, the doctor came to Charlotte's room with the discharge instructions. "I'm going to tell you how you are going to get better. Wear that brace no matter what, even sleep with it on and eat pizza and ice cream."

That's exactly what Charlotte did. After six months of wearing the brace and regular visits to the doctor, she healed completely, and her doctor was amazed. "I cannot believe you got back so fast!" he told her.

Charlotte had worn her hair in a bun for years, but with her neck in a brace, she had her hairstylist cut it short into a stylish bob so she wouldn't have to bother putting it up every day.

One day, she ran into someone who had not seen her for a while. "What happened to you? You look so young!" they told her.

Charlotte laughed and replied, "If you want to look younger, break your neck!"

CHAPTER 14

Remarkable Reunion

After breakfast, as part of her morning routine, Charlotte went into her spare bedroom and turned on her computer. She thought she would check her emails and take a quick peek on Facebook before she started running errands. She noticed that she had a message waiting for her, so she clicked on the icon. When it opened, she could barely believe what she was seeing:

> *hello lotte*
> *je suis Alain le petit garçon de Beaumont-en-Argonne*
> *depuis longtemps on espérait de tes nouvelles*
> *mes parents sont décédés depuis déjà longtemps*
> *mais ici on pense encore à toi*
> *on vient juste ce soir de me communiquer ton nom*
>
> *hello lotte*
> *I am Alain the little boy from Beaumont in Argonne*
> *for a long time we hoped to hear from you*
> *my parents died a long time ago*
> *but here we still think of you*
> *they just gave me your name tonight*

The name on the Facebook account that the message was coming from said Huberte Quatreville, but Alain obviously wrote the note! Charlotte rubbed her eyes as she couldn't believe what she had just read. She said out loud, "Am I dreaming?" She had not talked to Alain for more than 70 years.

"I didn't believe it on Facebook. It wasn't until he sent me a letter, and when I opened the letter, it sunk in that it was the Quatreville boy. I thought somebody found the name and sent it to me. I thought it was a fluke."

Charlotte called her daughter. "Roz, guess what?" Breathless, Charlotte felt her heart beating out of her chest.

"Mom, what is it?" Roz heard the excitement in her mother's voice and, for a moment, thought something bad had happened.

"I got a message from Alain Quatreville!"
Roz could hardly believe what she was hearing.

Charlotte explained what she had discovered when she opened Facebook Messenger.

"Mom, you have to write him back!"

Charlotte drafted a message back to Alain. She wanted to tell him what had happened since the last time she saw him. She had only returned once after the war to visit the Quatrevilles. Max and her father had come with her, but after their visit, they didn't keep in touch. She really wanted to put that dark part of her life behind her, and it took all her energy to take care of Max and help her father to rebuild his business and their lives.

"I was so moved; I couldn't believe that I was going to be in contact with him. I knew the mother and father had passed, but I couldn't believe that that little boy, who was four years old, would think about finding me."

Charlotte replied to Huberte, Alain's wife, who explained that Alain was not one to use the computer so she would be happy to relay any messages to her husband.

Through the correspondence, Charlotte learned that Alain was a math professor and had three grown children. He said he played with a doll named after her when she had left. He also shared that his parents were heartbroken that Charlotte had not kept in touch; they considered her a part of their family and talked about her often.

This information was hard for Charlotte to hear, but she explained how difficult her life was and knew at the time that the decision she made was the right one. She told him that she was so happy that he had found her and that she would really like to meet.

"I cannot wait to talk directly to him. When we talk or write I don't really feel that connection or that attachment."

Alain, 78, resided in Aiglemon, a village in France about 30 miles from Beaumont-en-Argonne. He didn't want to travel to the United States. He really wanted Charlotte to come to France. With Paris being about a three-hour train ride for him, he agreed to meet there.

Roz began planning a way for her family to travel with her mom to Paris. Her son Jeremy worked as director of product design at Facebook (now Meta). He shared his grandmother's Holocaust story and how Alain contacted her on Messenger with his co-workers in the Community Voices department. At that time, Community Voices' mission was to celebrate the people who bring the world closer together and find ways to lift each other up and support one another. Jeremy and the Community Voices team discussed documenting the reunion between Charlotte and Alain, and Facebook agreed to send along a crew to Paris to shoot video. Roz also set up a GoFundMe campaign to help raise funds, and many community members reached out when they heard about the trip.

"I don't know what he looks like; how will I know it's him when we meet?" Charlotte was worried and posed the question to Roz, who had come up with a plan about where the reunion should occur. She came up with the idea that her mom and

Alain should meet at the Shoah Memorial (Mémorial de la Shoah) in Paris. Charlotte had donated to the building fund of the museum and filled out the paperwork for her mother to be honored on its wall of names along with 76,000 Parisians who were killed during the Holocaust.

When Charlotte went to the museum's opening in 2005, she felt a wave of despair wash over her when she walked outside and saw the towering walls inscribed with names. "Oh Roz, I hope her name is not at the top!" she whispered to her daughter as they approached the monument. Charlotte, who stands 4 feet 6 inches, was overjoyed when they located Rose's name, which she could read at eye level.

Soon, in July 2018, Charlotte was back in Paris, at The Westin Paris Vendôme, waiting to go to meet the boy who she'd lived with so many decades earlier. As she and her brother Max chatted in the hotel lobby, she saw Roz talking to someone.

"Oh my God, oh my God," said Charlotte as she rushed across the room. There stood her former podiatrist and good friend, Dr. Michael Kates, and his wife, Elaine. Another family friend, Ashley Fleming, was also there. They had all traveled from Arizona to surprise Charlotte and to witness the reunion. Everyone embraced as the look of surprise stayed on Charlotte's face.

Another American had also come to surprise Charlotte. Elizabeth Blackburn met Charlotte, who became the topic of her thesis, when she was a journalism student at Arizona State University. She had become very close to the family. She had been in Kazakhstan and when she found out about the reunion, decided to travel to Paris to take part in the celebration. She also had a cousin who lived in England travel to Paris to join her, along with Madame Elazare's children, Harry, and Muriel, who still live in France.

Charlotte was so excited when they arrived at the Shoah Memorial the next day that she could barely contain herself. The Facebook camera crew was already in place, and so was Alain, sitting alone on a cement bench waiting for Charlotte.

Roz took her mother's arm, and they walked in silence through the memorial to the outside wall of names. Charlotte was wearing the shirt she liked to wear when she presented in public, the one with a photo of the Eiffel Tower on the front. Roz guided Charlotte to the four steps leading to the lower level, and as she walked carefully down the steps, she caught sight of Alain and smiled. As she approached, Alain's face lit up as he stood to greet her, and they embraced.

"What can I say, Charlotte?" were his first words as he rested his hand on her shoulder and kissed each of her cheeks.

Charlotte kept her hands on his arms, looked up into his eyes, and repeated, "This is a dream come true," over and over.

At the top of the stairs, Roz was overcome with emotion. She sobbed as she watched her mom come face to face with a member of the family who saved her life so long ago.

It was a gorgeous day, and the sun shone brightly as Charlotte showed Alain her mother's name on the wall. She put her hand to her lips and ran her fingers lightly over it.

"When I first saw him in France, you don't attach your-self right away when you don't know a person, so I was a little bit distant with him. He said, 'No, no, we are family.' It was really something special."

Charlotte asked Alain if he wanted to participate in the ritual she would always do when visiting the memorial. "Would you help me light a candle for my mother?"

As she held the candle in her trembling hand, Alain whispered, "Don't worry, I am with you," as they put the match flame to the candle's wick together.

Afterward, Alain told Charlotte he had something special that he wanted to share with her. He opened his backpack and took out a worn scrapbook. Inside were photos from when Charlotte and Max visited the Quatrevilles that one time after the war.

"Inside were photos of me and my brother and the family, the church and home, the grandmother, father, mother, Alain, and friends."

After the group left the museum, they met Alain's family for lunch. As they were getting ready to depart, after enjoying great food and each other's company, Alain posed a question. "My sister, who is 93, is paralyzed, and when she heard I was going to meet you … she said she would like to see you." He knew this was a big request to ask Charlotte and her family to travel so far to see Ginette, but he would never have forgiven himself if he didn't ask.

Roz looked at her mom. After all, this was her trip. If she wanted to go, Roz would make it happen.

Charlotte locked eyes with Alain and said, "Let's go see Ginette!"

Roz managed to procure a passenger van and driver, and the next day, Charlotte and her entourage piled in and set out on the three-hour drive to see Ginette. Since it was so close, they also planned on visiting Beaumont-en-Argonne.

In the van, Charlotte tried to mentally prepare herself before they arrived in the village where she had been hidden so many decades before. Like Alain and Ginette, many of the original occupants of the town during the war had moved, unable to walk the same streets where so many atrocities had occurred.

"Look, Mom!" Roz nudged her mom as they pulled up to the crowd gathered in the town square. Alain had notified some people ahead of time, and they had put up a notice on the church's bulletin board that "the girl hidden in the cellar during the war" would be arriving that day.

As Charlotte stepped out of the van, several people embraced her, the faces of adults now looking at her that she previously had etched in her mind as children.

Michel Piquard, the baker's son who had a crush on her, was among the first to greet Charlotte. "I remember I kissed her and never saw her again," he recounted to laughter from the crowd.

Christine Dollard-Leplomb gifted Charlotte with a book she had written in 2006, *Sauveteurs d'etoiles en Ardennes* [*Star rescuers in the Ardennes*] that had a section on the Quatrevilles and how they had hidden Charlotte.

A reporter from the town's newspaper also covered the event and featured Charlotte on the cover the next day.

"This reunion would have meant so much to my mother; she would have been so happy," reflected Alain as he stood glancing at his childhood home across the square. He also wanted Charlotte to know how traumatized he was from his grandmother shoving the bar of soap in his mouth to keep him from giving away her hiding space to the Nazi soldier. "That was awful!" he said.

"I want to see where I was hidden," said Charlotte. Alain took her arm to steady her on the cobblestone street and walked towards the house.

"That's the place where they killed people for hiding Jews," said Charlotte, pointing to the Église Saint-Jean-Baptiste. The Catholic church is the only building to remain untouched after the war, with bullet holes still visible in its stone walls. It stands as a reminder of the horrors this tiny village endured at the hands of the Germans.

As they approached the old home and post office, Charlotte recognized the outline of the stone building but little else. The house had been remodeled and had bright white shutters and a front door with numerous pots containing vibrant red geraniums lining the front wall.

"I felt very emotional when I saw the house. I was treated like gold. It was like my home; they were like my parents. Not too many survivors can go back to where they were."

The two stood on the doorstep and rang the bell. Charlotte felt her heart racing a little as the reality of where she was standing struck her. A man opened the door and wasn't overly friendly, so Alain quickly explained the meaning of their visit.

While the men were talking, Charlotte glanced inside. Even though the main room had been remodeled, memories came flooding back to her of the time spent in that very room: where she slept when she wasn't in hiding; where she was almost discovered by the Germans that evening with Robert; and where she finally came up from the dark cellar when the Americans came.

Charlotte snapped out of her daydream as the man responded, "It won't be possible to come in; the owner is ill." With that, he closed the door on the two of them.

Charlotte and Alain exchanged surprised glances, and both agreed they should leave.

"What happened?" Roz asked after witnessing the short interaction from the street.

"I guess we won't be going in," Charlotte shrugged.

Instead, the group continued walking through the village, with Alain pointing out the various places that Charlotte frequented the short time she was above ground in the Ardennes.

Roz was amazed as they walked to see the stories she heard growing up about her mother's time in Beaumont-en-Argonne coming to life before her.

"Mom, everything you told me as a child about your time here was just as you described. I now have seen it with my own eyes," said Roz. She was so happy to be able to share this incredible experience, not only with her mom but with her husband and sons, too. "It will be etched in our minds and hearts forever," she said.

The group then traveled the short distance to Ginette's home, and while the others were chatting, Charlotte sat silent, lost in thought.

"Ginette was like a mother to me, so if I see her, I'm afraid that it's going to make me feel bad...that she's not the Ginette she was. She was always running around. She was running the house because her mother was busy with the post office, and her father was busy with the farm."

When they arrived at Ginette's home, Alain took Charlotte's arm and guided her through the front door. Charlotte entered the brightly lit room and greeted Ginette's two daughters and saw the woman past them propped up on pillows in a hospital bed. Ginette's eyes lit up when she recognized the girl she used to take care of in the cellar. Charlotte went over and took her hand and gingerly kissed Ginette on the cheek, tasting the salt of her tears as she wept openly.

Although she was physically paralyzed, Ginette's mind was sharp. The two women visited for a while, reminiscing, and Charlotte asked her if she had ever married Robert, the boyfriend who caused the only cross words shared between them. Ginette smiled and said, "No."

"She was my main girl; she took care of me. She gave me a little bit of life. If it weren't for her, I would be like a dog. Ginette was fantastic. I thanked her for taking care of me when I was in hiding."

When Charlotte walked out of the house, her heart was full, and she was so glad they'd made the drive to see Ginette, who died a year later.

They went back to Beaumont-en-Argonne to say goodbye, and Charlotte expressed to all who came out to greet her how meaningful it was, "I will never forget this," she told them.

When they returned to the hotel that night, mother and daughter talked about what an emotional day it had been. Roz said, "Mom, I can't believe that you were in that village."

Charlotte replied, "I told you kids that story; now it was proven."

"Sometimes I have dreams, and I'm back right there. I wake up and think, 'Oh it's just a dream.' I tell the school kids when I tell my story. I go to bed with it; I wake up with it. It's always there. The Germans didn't get me, but they branded me. The stories are right there."

The next day, the family planned to celebrate Max's 80th birthday. His wife never celebrated birthdays, so since Charlotte was in France, she insisted that Max spend his birthday with them so they could spend the day and have a nice dinner.

"*Joyeux anniversaire!*" Charlotte greeted her brother as they met in the hotel lobby.

"*Merci,*" responded Max.

Their first stop that morning was to visit their father's grave in the Cimetiere Parisien de Bagneux.

"In Paris, they don't have too much room for burying people, so my father is buried with the people from his village where he was born. You have to have a fortune to get a main tombstone in Paris. The people from Poland didn't think of having their own tombstone; they wanted to be among their fellow villagers."

Just like she had done at the Mémorial de la Shoah, Charlotte put her fingers to her lips and then on the photo of her father. "I love you, Papa," she said.

Max took a moment to reminisce about their childhood before the war and then about how hard their father had to work to make their life whole again after the war.

"He was so good to us," Charlotte said as she fought back tears.

They walked arm in arm while the rest of the family hung back, letting the siblings have their time together. Max's wife would not allow him to come to the States to visit Charlotte, and she figured, at 86, this would probably be her last trip to Paris.

They next went to visit the place where the orphanage used to be, where the nightmare really began. With the grandeur of the Sacré-Coeur in the distance, the family stood in silence, reading the plaque about the 79 children that had been picked up and taken to Auschwitz.

"We could have been one of the children on this plaque," Charlotte said. Max looked at her and nodded as tears welled up in his eyes. Charlotte embraced her brother and the two stood there for a bit, crying, and holding each other.

"We don't talk too much about the past, but when we do, he says, 'Charlotte, do you feel again what happened to us during the war?' And I say, 'I have it when I get up and when I go to bed,' and he said, 'I have it too.' He cannot forget what happened. When you get hit like that, especially at a young age, it's a terrible blow."

"This is hardly a way to spend a birthday," Charlotte said, wiping the tears from her face and offering Max a tissue. "No more tears, let's go celebrate."

They found a restaurant that could accommodate them all and ate, laughed, and toasted Max. Charlotte enjoyed a panaché, a draft beer mixed with carbonated lemonade.

"When I was little, they would put lemonade in the beer for kids to introduce us to drinking, and they'd put water in the wine." The taste reminded her of good times and celebrations.

Although it was a remarkable event that brought her to Paris, it hurt her to return to the city. "It reminds me of a lot of things about my mother and my father, but it's a beautiful city. It deserves to be seen."

As they checked out of the hotel the next day, the staff was sad to see Charlotte go. They had grown fond of her, and after hearing her story, they delivered flowers, fruit, and juices every day to her room, and one day, they even sent champagne.

Upon returning to Arizona, Roz and Charlotte set out to see how they could get the Quatrevilles, Alain's parents, recognized at Yad Vashem, The World Holocaust Remembrance Center in Jerusalem, Israel. The center has a section that honors non-Jews who risked their lives to save Jews during the Holocaust, referred to as the "Righteous."

With the help of a priest in Phoenix and Kim Klett, an English teacher who has been teaching a class in Holocaust literature to high schoolers for more than 20 years and whose students Charlotte has spoken to on multiple occasions, Roz was able to finish the lengthy paperwork process required by Yad Vashem.

On March 27, 2019, André and Léa Quatreville were officially recognized and their names were commemorated in the Garden of the Righteous Among the Nations at Yad Vashem in Israel. On April 11, 2019, in Beaumont-en-Argonne, Alain and Huberte attended a ceremony and Alain was presented with a certificate of honor and a medal on his parents' behalf.

Charlotte and Alain continue to correspond via Facebook Messenger, and phone calls. She revised her public presentation speech so that she could include the part about their reunion.

Charlotte has said that everyone always tells her that she is amazing and that she is always smiling. She tells them: "You know what? I am a survivor. If you want to survive, you survive. I say, 'I am smiling because I'm happy that I survived.'"

"I have a wonderful family. In all my talks at the end, I say, I have a message for you, 'Love your family, you have only one family in a lifetime, respect each other and be positive.' That is the best thing you can do in life."

THE END

PHOTO GALLERY

Reunion

Charlotte and Max visiting the orphanage, Paris

Charlotte and Max honoring their mother's
name at the Mémorial de la Shoah, Paris

Charlotte's family and friends visiting for the reunion of
Charlotte and the Quatrevilles, Paris, 2018

Charlotte reunites with Alain Quatreville at the
Mémorial de la Shoah, Paris, 2018

Charlotte with her grandchildren, Jeremy and Jacob,
at the Mémorial de la Shoah, Paris, 2018

Charlotte and Alain, Le Marais, Paris, 2018

Charlotte reunites with Ginette Quatreville, 2018

Charlotte meets Alain's family and the townspeople
of Beaumont en Argonne, 2018

Charlotte and Alain in front of the Quatreville's home
where she was hidden, Beaumont en Argonne, 2018

Charlotte, Paris

ABOUT THE AUTHOR

A native of Arizona, Mala Blomquist grew up in Scottsdale, where she gained an appreciation for the desert and a love of its breathtaking sunsets. As a young wife and mother, she began freelance writing, which spanned into a career as a writer and editor for niche publications in Arizona for more than 25 years. She currently resides in the Valley with her husband and an assortment of animals.

Made in United States
Troutdale, OR
04/07/2025